CITIES OF LEGEND

THE MYCENAEAN WORLD

Current and forthcoming titles in the Classical World Series

Classical World Series

CITIES OF LEGEND
THE MYCENAEAN WORLD

K.A. & Diana Wardle

Bristol Classical Press

General Editor: John H. Betts
Series Editor: Michael Gunningham

For Nicola
who shares our endless fascination

Cover illustration adapted from the Lion Gate at Mycenae

First published in 1997 by
Bristol Classical Press
an imprint of
Gerald Duckworth & Co. Ltd
61 Frith Street
London W1D 3JL
e-mail: inquiries@duckworth-publishers.co.uk
Website: www.ducknet.co.uk

Revised edition 2000

Reprinted 2001

A catalogue record for this book is available
from the British Library

ISBN 1-85399-355-7

Printed in Great Britain by
Antony Rowe Ltd

Contents

List of Illustrations

Abbreviations of sources:

Acknowledgements

We are grateful to Ben Willmore for preparing computer generated maps and diagrams, to Ken Dowden for his comments on Homer and Greek dialects, to John Prag and Richard Neave for the heads, and particularly to Lisa French for sharing her knowledge and her library, to Heinrich Schliemann, Georges Perrot and Charles Chipier, Christos Tsountas and J. Irving Manatt, Sir Arthur Evans, and Alan Wace for employing such excellent artists and illustrators, named and unnamed, that their work can be reproduced here.

Preface to the Second Edition

In preparing this edition we have taken the opportunity to add a brief chapter bibliography for those with access to a specialist library and an index to some of the principal topics, while the internet section has been expanded to take into account the rapidly increasing resources available.

K.A. & Diana Wardle
August 2000

The cities of the hero age thine eyes may seek in vain,
Save where some wrecks of ruin still break the level plain,
So once I saw Mycenae, the ill-starred, a barren height
Too bleak for goats to pasture, – the goat-herds point the site.
And as I passed a grey-beard said, 'Here used to stand of old
A city built by giants, and passing rich in gold'.

Alpheus, in *Anthologia Palatina*, ix, 101
translated by Rennell Rodd

Ivory head from the Room with the Fresco at Mycenae, ht 6.8cm, c. 1230 BC.

Chapter 1
Introduction

Mycenae stands out among the cities of legend celebrated in Homer's poetry as well-built, well-streeted or rich in gold, the royal seat of Agamemnon, leader of the Greek expedition against Troy. The great poems and the tradition of oral poetry may have only preserved the memory of the deeds of heroes, but the citadel of Mycenae itself was known and stood proud above the Argive plain for all to see, century after century. A small community sheltered within the walls throughout the Dark Age (12th to 8th centuries BC) until parts were demolished in the 5th century BC by the people of Argos, who saw Mycenae and its inhabitants as a threat to their own mastery of the region. The travel writer Pausanias while touring Greece in the 2nd century AD visited the citadel and was shown the royal graves. Travellers in later centuries reported the romantic ruin and sometimes searched for antiquities, but few made much of the association between the heroic deeds and the ancient fortress.

It remained for the German magnate Heinrich Schliemann to demonstrate the connection and to begin to identify the flourishing civilization known today as Mycenaean. His financial resources and an obsession with the belief that the legends were true spurred him not only to excavate at Troy but at Mycenae, Tiryns and Orchomenos as well. His discovery at Mycenae, in 1876, of the royal Shaft Graves (see Chapter 2) with their vast quantities of gold, weapons and exotic imports attracted the attention of all – scholars, politicians and the public – and made certain that archaeologists would continue to explore the achievements of the prehistoric civilization echoed in the Homeric epic.

This Mycenaean civilization lasted for about 500 years – from the first burials in the Shaft Graves at Mycenae, c.1600 BC, to its final disappearance, c.1050 BC. During this period its nature altered and its influence increased rapidly. The first Mycenaean tombs, pottery and other artefacts belong to the 16th century and are confined to the Peloponnese, Attica and Central Greece. By the 13th century Mycenaean Greece extended northwards to Mount Olympus and the Ambracian Gulf, eastwards to the Dodecanese and south to Crete – an area which corresponds well with the origin of the Achaean hosts as set out in 'the

Fig. 1 Map of Late Bronze Age Greece with principal sites mentioned in text.

catalogue of ships' (*Iliad* II). Mycenaean contacts, however, extended much further: from the coast of Egypt and Syria in the east, to Macedonia and the Black Sea in the north and to Italy and even Spain in the west.

It is impossible to explain all the complexities of Mycenaean civilization in a brief introduction such as this book. Our intention is to provide a framework for further reading, whether as part of a Classical Civilization course at School or College, or an introduction to the Greek Bronze Age at University level. It is not our aim to include a detailed discussion of the Homeric references or an examination of 'Homeric' society but rather to enable the student to appreciate the background against which the epic may be read. For the Greeks of the Classical period the Homeric epics *were* history, to be taken at face value. Since then opinions about the historicity of the epics have ranged from total scepticism to total acceptance. Were Agamemnon, Achilles, Odysseus and Priam real people who ruled in the early Greek world we are about to describe or were they the products of a fertile imagination, used to give life and verisimilitude to stories of heroic deeds and heroic endurance? For us and, we hope, for our readers the first priority is to try and understand the Mycenaean world in its own right and then, and *only* then to see where the epics belong – to see how much is fact and how much fantasy.

We have started with an outline of the rise and fall of Mycenaean civilization, (Chapter 2): there were many changes during its five hundred year span. Many regional variations also existed but they are beyond our scope. We shall 'visit' a number of sites in this study and we have included brief descriptions of the most important of these (Chapter 3) to help readers find their way around. Knowledge of the early Mycenaean period derives from tombs and the finds in them (Chapter 4) and these continue to provide much information throughout the Mycenaean era. The objects found in them illustrate many aspects of the art and craftsmanship developed and maintained in Greece (Chapter 5).

In the 13th century BC, when there is most information about fortresses, palaces and settlements, a complex economy and social structure existed in those areas where palace centres had become established – the Argolid, Messenia, Thebes, Gla and Western Crete. From this period too comes most of the evidence contained on the clay tablets written in the script called Linear B which uses an early form of the Greek language found in Mycenaean palaces and other sites.

These two main sources of information enable us to visualize the basic elements of the economy and social organization (Chapter 6). The successful exploitation of the landscape for agricultural production allowed manpower to be mustered for major public works (Chapter 7), or for military purposes (Chapter 8). Vivid wall-paintings in the palaces and other buildings provide images of the Mycenaeans as they saw themselves (Chapter 9). The economic success of the Mycenaean palaces both depended on and fostered trade over a wide area of the Mediterranean (Chapter 10). Cult and religious beliefs must have played a large part in the shape of this society and the names of some of the gods of the Olympian pantheon were already in use. However, the exact nature of their beliefs and the role of the objects which accompanied cult practice remain enigmatic (Chapter 11).

The very complexity, even artificiality, of the system, perhaps contributed to its demise. The upheavals and destructions at the end of the 13th century, whatever their cause, were sufficient to sweep it away beyond recall. Although Greece in the 12th century still used Mycenaean artefacts and the basic agricultural economy was unchanged, the structure of its society was probably based on numerous petty chiefdoms. It was these which continued into the Dark Age and provided the immediate inspiration for the rival warrior lords described in the Homeric epic (Chapter 12). Some of the detail, and even some of the stories, may originate during that Dark Age. The traditional date for Homer's life falls at the end of this period, i.e., the end of the 8th century BC.

Illustration, in a book of this size, must inevitably be restricted and the reader may find some surprising omissions. We have rejected some well known objects which are frequently reproduced (often in colour) in favour of those illustrations which are explanatory. These may readily be supplemented by the books and guides we have included in the suggestions for further reading. The best way to understand the achievements of Mycenaean civilization is to visit Greece, her principal historic sites and her major museums. The Mycenaean Room of the National Museum at Athens has recently been refurbished and provides a vivid picture of the wealth and variety of Mycenaean trade and manufactures. Other exhibitions well worth seeing can be found in Nauplion in the Argolid, Chora in Messenia and Thebes in Boeotia. Nearer to home, the British Museum has a good collection of Mycenaean objects, with smaller collections in the Ashmolean Museum, Oxford and the Manchester University Museum.

Chapter 2
The rise and fall of Mycenaean civilization

When?

All too often, in the shorter accounts, Mycenaean civilization appears to be treated as a single, uniform entity with little development in time and little variation in space. The achievements described in this book may already be over three thousand years old, but they occupy a period of some five hundred years between c.1600 and 1050 BC as set out in the table below. Three broad divisions of this period will suffice for our purpose:- the **Early Mycenaean** period (16th-15th centuries BC), best known for the Shaft Graves at Mycenae; the **Palatial** period (14th and 13th centuries), which we have used to denote the period from which the remains of palaces do survive (without meaning to imply there were none before this); and **Late Mycenaean** (12th and 11th centuries BC), a period of temporary recovery following the destructions which swept away the Palaces and the administrative system they supported. Two strands of information provide the time-scale against which can be set the monumental fortifications, palaces and tombs and the objects of bronze and ivory, stone and clay which the Mycenaeans made and used.

Relative chronology is obtained from sequences of pottery. This, the most abundant and durable of Mycenaean artefacts, was well made and often elaborately decorated. Fashions and style changed rapidly so that the products of different periods can be easily recognised. The *stratigraphy* of successive levels found in careful excavations and the analyses of the pottery in each level enable us to place this pottery in the correct, *relative* order. In this way, whole pots or groups of broken sherds found on the palace floors or in tombs can be correctly placed in the sequence of development.

Absolute chronology has been established by linking these sequences to Egyptian sites and finds. In Egypt, the elaborate records which the rulers caused to be kept and the few exact correspondences between these written records and rare astronomical phenomena (of the same kind as Halley's Comet) have enabled the construction of an historical chronology for the period when Mycenaean civilization flourished, which is generally

Date BC		Principal events on mainland	Principal sites and discoveries		Principal events elsewhere
2000		Middle Bronze Age			Old Palaces in Crete
					Linear A
					Troy VI
					Hyksos in Egypt
1650		Tumuli	Grave Circle B		New Palaces in Crete
					Akrotiri
1600		Mycenaean pottery	Grave Circle A		Thera Eruption
	E	Shaft Graves		L	
		Tholoi in Messenia			
1500	A	Chamber tombs		A	
		Tholoi widespread	Vapheio		Tuthmosis III
	R			T	
1450					
	L			E	
1425			Dendra Armour		Destruction of Minoan
	Y				Palaces
1400		Early Palaces	Menelaion	B	Amenophis III
		Wall-paintings	Tiryns, Thebes		Linear B at Knossos
1375	P			R	Destruction of Knossos
					(high date)
1350	A		Treasury of Atreus ?	O	Akhenaten
			Treasury of Minyas		Tell el-Amarna
	L			N	Tutankhamun
1316			Kaş Wreck		
1300	A	Later palaces	Assiros granary	Z	
			Thebes 'treasury'		
1250	T			E	Ramesses II
		Cyclopean Walls at	Copais drained ?		Destruction of Knossos
	I	Mycenae, Athens,	Gla built		(low date)
		Tiryns, Midea etc.	Mycenae Cult Centre	A	
	A	? Trojan War ?			
		Linear B	Gelidonya Wreck	G	Linear B at Chania
	L				
1200		Palaces destroyed		E	Troy VII

(Left margin bracket: E A R L Y · P A L A T I A L; right margin bracket: L A T E · B R O N Z E · A G E)

Fig. 2 Mycenaean Greece: events, sites and parallels 2000-1200 BC.

accurate to within a few years. The archaeologist can use the patterns of Mycenaean trade and contact to transfer these Egyptian dates to Greece. When, for example, Mycenaean pottery is found in buildings in Egypt or Egyptian scarabs (beetle-shaped seals carrying the name or title of a Pharaoh) are found in Greece with Mycenaean pottery, the pottery itself can be dated quite accurately and the date thus established transferred to the relative sequence.

In the last twenty years, scientific methods of dating – carbon 14 and dendrochronology – have begun to provide *absolute* dates for events in the Mycenaean period, independently of pottery or Egyptian history. The technique of dendrochronology, which counts the annual growth rings of trees – one ring equals one year – in timber which has survived as charcoal, promises, in the near future, to yield dates accurate to within a year or two. These can be used to check or revise those derived from pottery and its associations. Some recent studies suggest that the date for the beginning of the Mycenaean period may need to be revised upwards by as much as 70 years, but we have employed the chronology based on the Egyptian records to avoid confusion until the matter is resolved.

In contrast, neither Homer nor the other literary sources of Classical Greece give us firm dates for events in the heroic past. Even the different dates for the Trojan war given by Herodotus and Eratosthenes depend on counting generations back from their own day. Generations, indeed, had often been invented to link noble families with divine or heroic ancestors.

Finer divisions of the Mycenaean period to be found in more detailed accounts are based on the style of pottery in use at each stage: for example 'Late Helladic (LH) IIIB' is the name given to the pottery in use at the height of Mycenaean prosperity in the 13th century BC. These divisions have, however, no necessary connection with major historical changes. Pottery reflects the taste of potters in the first place and that of their customers second, though it may sometimes reflect general economic circumstances in its quality or elaboration.

We have set out the principal events and sites within Mycenaean Greece and linked them to those in Egypt and neighbouring areas in the chart opposite; this is continued from 1200 BC onwards in Fig. 38 (p. 122).

The Early Mycenaean period (16th-15th centuries).

The origins of Mycenaean civilization have been much debated. That the Mycenaeans were Greek is beyond question, since the decipherment of the clay tablets from the palatial period with the Linear B script showed them to be inscribed in an early form of Greek. *When* they came to Greece, if they were not indigenous, is still uncertain. It is clear that they descend from the inhabitants of southern Greece in the Middle Bronze Age (2000-1600 BC), as many of their burial customs, their weapons and the shapes and decoration of their pottery derive from those of that period. Their wealth and contacts were increasing at the same time as the Minoans in Crete (who had had a sophisticated literate society since 2000 BC) began to take a greater interest in trade with their neighbours in the Aegean sea and on the mainland. The resulting mixture of 'native' traditions and 'imported' ideas as well as artefacts can be seen in the rich burials in the Shaft Graves at Mycenae as well as in the early *tholos* tombs (built circular tombs) of Messenia in the SW Peloponnese. Ideas and raw materials were also derived from the north and west.

Minoan Crete

The history and achievements of the Minoan civilization of Crete are a separate story, but in the early Mycenaean period the two areas are closely linked and it is frequently impossible – and indeed usually pointless – to try to separate Minoan from Mycenaean. The palatial centres of Crete had suffered destruction – perhaps as a result of an earthquake – towards the end of the Middle Bronze Age, c.1650 BC, but had been rebuilt on the same scale and continued to flourish in what is known as the 'New Palace' period. Characteristic features of Minoan civilization include the administrative records, kept in a language as yet undeciphered (Linear A), the scale and quality of their palatial architecture, their wall-paintings, elaborate stone vessels and intricately decorated sealstones, as well as pottery decorated in a lively, often naturalistic style. Although we are well informed about their palaces, towns and villages, very few burials of the New Palace period have been found. This is in contrast to the picture of the early stages of Mycenaean civilization where the evidence is almost entirely from tombs. Outside Crete, Minoan contact can be seen clearly in communities in the Aegean islands of Kythera, Melos, Aegina, Kea, Thera and Rhodes but this did not amount to domination. Minoan trade at this period extended as far as Egypt and Italy.

The buried town of Akrotiri on Thera

Excavations at Akrotiri on the island of Thera, the southernmost island of the Cyclades, have begun to uncover a town of the same period as the Shaft Graves buried around 1550 BC by volcanic ash and pumice from one of the largest eruptions to have occurred in man's recent history. As at Pompeii, this eruption has preserved a vivid picture of life in a flourishing town, with its houses still standing two and three storeys in height, with brilliantly coloured wall-paintings still in position and with many objects abandoned when the inhabitants fled. The cosmopolitan nature of the objects found confirms that this was an independent community whose prosperity was based on seafaring – as illustrated in a wall-painting in the West House (Chapter 9) – and trade with Crete, Egypt, the Eastern Mediterranean as well as with mainland Greece.

Mainland Greece

Minoan civilization and the town at Akrotiri both flourished during the first stages of Mycenaean civilization. The best-known finds of this period were made in the Shaft Graves discovered by Schliemann in Grave Circle A at Mycenae itself, which were clearly the royal burials of an extraordinarily wealthy dynasty. Gold face masks, dress ornaments and jewellery covered the bodies. The dead were provided with vessels of gold and silver and weapons in profusion to equip them for the next life. A second grave circle (B), further from the citadel, contained similar, though less wealthy burials of earlier date. We can hardly imagine the quantity of precious objects available to the Mycenaeans if they felt able to devote this much to the dead. These and other graves were clearly outside the walls of the citadel. However, no trace of these early walls survived the construction nearly three hundred years later of the massive walls that can be seen today. In the same way little is known of the nature of any palace these wealthy rulers might have occupied. Other sites in the Argolid, besides Mycenae, confirm that this was one of the earliest and most prosperous areas of Mycenaean Greece.

A second area where early finds have been made is Messenia in the south west of the Peloponnese. Here burials in large *tumuli* (mounds) and later in the first of the monumental tholos tombs were accompanied by gold vessels and inlaid daggers like those from Mycenae as well as jewellery of amber and other precious materials. Early Mycenaean finds have also been made in Laconia and Corinth, Athens and Marathon, Thebes and Orchomenos, Kirrha and Krisa near Delphi, and in coastal Thessaly. At this period the Mycenaeans were already in contact with coastal Macedonia, Albania and Italy as shown by finds of their pottery and weapons.

The character of Mycenaean society at this point is still uncertain. It is likely, as for the whole Mycenaean period, that each district was independent of the next and had its own local ruler. Mycenae may have exercised some hegemony, as Agamemnon does over the other leaders in the *Iliad*, but it was never a 'capital' in any modern sense.

Expansion and maturity

As Mycenaean civilization began to spread, shaft graves and tumuli went out of use. They were replaced by ever larger and more elaborate tholoi for kings and princes, and *chamber tombs* (tombs with a square or circular chamber cut into a hill slope), which were multiple tombs for the wealthier families in each community. These tombs often have individual finds just as rich as those from earlier graves, though rarely in the same quantity – gold vessels and rings, weapons and even armour. The earliest known European armour – a full cuirass in bronze – was found in such a chamber tomb at Dendra, a few kilometres south of Mycenae. We still know very little about how people lived – as opposed to how they died – since so few buildings have been discovered. A mansion or small palace existed near Sparta at the site later used for a sanctuary dedicated to Helen and Menelaus. Early fragments of wall-paintings from Tiryns and Mycenae hint at the predecessors of the 13th-century BC palaces. Only at Pylos have sections of the fortification wall been discovered, though the choice of hill-top sites for Mycenaean settlement indicates a strong concern for defence.

The eruption of the Thera volcano c.1550 cannot have gone unnoticed in mainland Greece, yet no traces of its effects have been found there. The destruction of the majority of the Minoan palaces c.1425 was, however, of considerable significance for the mainlanders. The causes of this destruction remain unclear: the Mycenaeans are often said to have been responsible. Chamber tombs and weapon burials, typical of the mainland, first appear after the destruction, while the archives at Knossos, the only palace to survive these destructions, are written in Linear B in Greek. More importantly, the Mycenaeans were now able to dominate the whole of the southern Aegean and take over the former Minoan trade in the Eastern Mediterranean. From now on, Mycenaean pottery, not Minoan, is found in Egypt, Syria and Cyprus.

The Palatial period (14th-13th centuries)

The early part of this period sees the construction of the last and largest of the tholos tombs such as the 'Treasury of Atreus' at Mycenae and 'Treasury of Minyas' at Orchomenos in Boeotia. Sadly, these prominent monuments were already robbed in antiquity and give us little idea about the wealth of their contents. By the middle of the 13th century the great citadels of Mycenae, Tiryns and Midea in the Argolid and of Athens and of Gla in Boeotia had massive 'Cyclopean' fortification walls, built from such large stones that they were thought in antiquity to have been the work of giants – the Cyclopes. Palaces have been discovered at Mycenae, Tiryns and Pylos – the last apparently unfortified – as well as suspected at Athens on the Acropolis and at Thebes under the modern town. Wall-paintings are common at palatial sites, but fragments have also been found in domestic contexts and tombs. An archive of Linear B tablets from Pylos illuminates many aspects of Mycenaean palace adminstration. Further tablets have been found at Mycenae, Tiryns and Thebes. There is more evidence for towns and ordinary houses at this period but nothing explored yet to compare with towns excavated in Crete, such as Gournia and Palaikastro.

The Mycenaean palatial centres, at least, were fully involved in Mediterranean trade, importing raw materials such as copper, tin and ivory, exporting perfumes, woollen cloth and perhaps manpower. The clearest evidence of this trade can be seen in the abundant Mycenaean pottery at the Egyptian city of Tell el-Amarna (the new capital built by the heretical Pharaoh Akhenaten, who reigned for over fifteen years in the middle of the 14th century BC). Exploration of the western Mediterranean may have included colonies in southern Italy and reached Sardinia, perhaps even Spain.

Mycenaean Crete?

Following the destructions of the Minoan palaces c.1425 BC, Mycenaean influence in Crete was at first very strong. Soon, however, Cretan characteristics in burial habits, pottery style and other artefacts began to re-emerge. This may be connected with the final destruction of the palace at Knossos, which some see as a Mycenaean administrative centre. The date of Knossos' destruction by fire is, however, disputed. Sir Arthur Evans thought the fierce conflagration took place early in the 14th century, but recent evidence, particularly from the use of the Linear B script there, has called this date into question. Some scholars would like to bring the destruction into the 13th century, with as yet unassessed consequences for our understanding of Crete in this period. Even if the continuing use of a palace at Knossos in the 13th century is in question, there is no doubt that there was one at Chania (ancient Kydonia) in western Crete, where numbers of Linear B tablets have been found in the remains of a large building under the modern town.

The Trojan War

Although the story of the Trojan War is in great part the product of poetic imagination, Homer's epics include enough circumstantial detail to confirm that memories of a bronze age world are embedded in the poems. This gives us confidence to accept the historicity of the central theme – an expedition by a large Greek force, united temporarily under a single powerful leader, Agamemnon, to attack the great fortress of Troy. The archaeological record shows that Mycenaean Greece was at its most influential and, perhaps, most united in the 13th century BC. Not for another seven hundred years would the inhabitants of Greece have once again the capacity to mount an expedition on the scale reflected in Homer's *Iliad*. Attempts by archaeologists to find proof of the sack in the ruins of Troy itself are inconclusive. The city suffered destruction and was rebuilt many times over a period of three thousand years until finally abandoned in the late Roman era. Of the nine major periods into which the strata reflecting its history can be divided, two are contemporary with Mycenaean civilization – Troy VI and Troy VIIa. Troy VI was a fine city with massive walls, broad streets and imposing buildings, fit for a Priam, but seems to have been brought low by earthquake rather than enemy action. Troy VIIa, a mere shadow of its predecessor, was indeed destroyed by fire but this occurred in the 12th century not the 13th.

The Late Mycenaean period (12th-11th centuries)

Round about 1200 the palaces were destroyed and were not rebuilt. The palatial administration disappeared together with most of the attributes of the palaces. There is no evidence, for example, for wall-paintings or elaborate architecture (with the possible exception of reconstruction at Tiryns), and a much reduced production of luxury goods. The cause is just as much a puzzle as that of the earlier destructions of the Minoan palaces. These events coincided with major upheavals in the Eastern Mediterranean such as the incursions of the 'Sea Peoples' into Egypt and the partial collapse of the Hittite empire. In Greece, it is no longer enough, as used to be the case, to blame the Dorians of the Classical tradition as invaders from the north because there is nothing tangible to mark their coming.

In the aftermath of the destruction of the Palaces, the uniformity of Mycenaean civilization began to fragment, though there was a partial recovery of prosperity. Regional styles of pottery and local preferences in burial practice became more and more marked, but both continue established traditions. The great citadel walls still gave protection at several sites. Rich grave offerings were still made occasionally and elaborate pottery was again manufactured on a limited scale. Yet the recovery was short-lived. Economic decline set in so that by the middle of the 11th century BC there was little left which can be called 'Mycenaean'. The heroic age was over – but the memory of its riches and its deeds were preserved in oral poetry and tradition throughout the Dark Age for Homer to immortalise in his epic works.

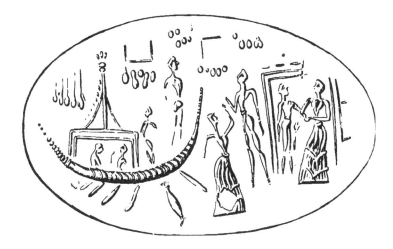

Fig. 3 Gold ring from the Tiryns Treasure. This scene, showing a couple in a doorway and the same (?) couple moving towards a boat with mast and oars, with a town and onlookers in the background(?), will have represented a story familiar to its wearer. It may even have depicted a story preserved in later Greek mythology, such as the departure of Theseus and Ariadne from Crete, or the abduction of Helen by Paris which caused the Trojan war. Today we speculate on its meaning and marvel at the imagery portrayed in a space no more than 3.4cm across.

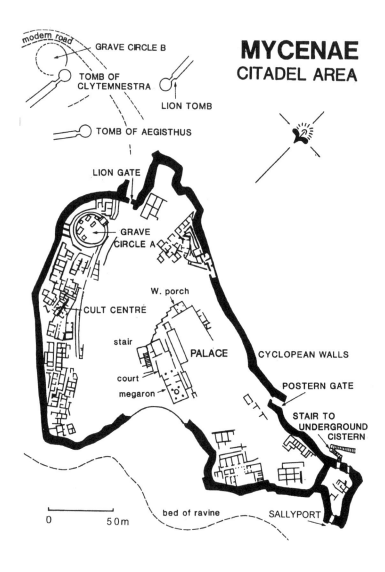

Fig. 4 Mycenae: the citadel and adjacent areas in c. 1200 BC.

Chapter 3
Cities

The 'catalogue of ships' in Book 2 of the *Iliad*, with its details of the numbers and origin of the ships assembled for the expedition against Troy, matches the distribution of the principal Mycenaean sites in southern Greece. Some, as in Messenia, were no longer important centres when Homer created his epic. The number of ships and men supplied by each of Agamemnon's allies corresponds singularly well with the potential of each district and so is far from poetic licence. Either Homer had an excellent knowledge of geography and resources or some remarkably accurate memories had survived to his day. Mycenaean sites, great and small, share similar characteristics. They each focus on a fortified citadel in a commanding position, close to water and good agricultural land, often within reach of the sea. Their subsequent history, of course, is varied: some places, like Mycenae, became little more than villages, whilst at Athens building in the Archaic and Classical periods has removed most traces of the heroic age. Archaeological research and the chance of discovery are both so uneven that each site presents us with a different, sometimes unconnected part of the picture of a Mycenaean community and its achievements.

Argos

In the Mycenaean period Argos was a minor centre, perhaps controlling the routes from the Argive plain across the mountains to Arcadia. Its remains include substantial buildings and numerous chamber tombs, as well as a tholos tomb in the vicinity. It is only at the end of the Mycenaean period that Argos became and remained the most important city of the Argolid. The tragedian Aeschylus echoes the former relationship between Mycenae and Argos when the inhabitants of Mycenae are addressed as 'Argives' (people of Argos).

Athens

Little remains to show the importance of the capital of Erechtheus and

Menestheus, legendary kings of Athens, about 10km. from the sea in the centre of the western Attica plain. Its Cyclopean walls around the Acropolis probably survived until the Persian sack of 480 BC. A few traces can still be found, together with the rock-cut staircase which led down into a cleft in the rock on the west side of the Acropolis to reach a protected water supply. A few Mycenaean chamber tombs and one tholos at Menidi in the northern outskirts of modern Athens have survived centuries of building activities.

Nothing is known of the fate of Athens in the destructions of c.1200 BC. Yet the city remained a flourishing centre and was one of the most prosperous communities of the Dark Age and later. Tradition asserted that the people of Athens were indigenous, not newcomers.

Ithaca

Despite the efforts that have gone into the search for Ithaca – on the island itself or on the neighbouring islands of Lefkas or Kephallenia – little has been found to represent the kingdom of wily Odysseus. There are Mycenaean sites on the island, including the Polis cave located in a position that matches the Homeric description of Odysseus' first return, but so far no monumental buildings and no tombs have been found. The adjacent island of Kephallenia, which also formed part of Odysseus' kingdom, has large chamber tomb cemeteries, chiefly of 12th-century date. The Dark Age is perhaps better represented with offerings in the Polis cave – including fragments of bronze tripod-stands like those Odysseus had concealed – and at the Aetos sanctuary not far away. These offerings reflect the adventurers and traders who explored the routes to Italy from the 9th century BC onwards and regarded Odysseus as their protector, honouring him when setting out or in gratitude for a safe return.

Iolkos

The kingdom of Jason, leader of the Argonauts, centred on the port of Iolkos at the head of the Magnesian gulf in Thessaly. Substantial Mycenaean remains have been found here – under the modern town of Volos – and there are a number of tombs in the vicinity. An alternative candidate for the ancient town of Iolkos is some 5km. further inland at Dimini where there are two impressive tholos tombs and a Mycenaean town. This area continued to be important during the succeeding Dark Age.

Knossos

This, the most famous of the Cretan cities with the palace of King Minos at its heart, alone survived the series of destructions around 1425 BC which brought to an end the Cretan palace civilization. The Mycenaeans may have been the culprits, sacking the other palaces but retaining Knossos as the administrative centre of their new possession. In any case their influence is clear. This great palace, with its central and western courtyards and rows of storerooms for grain and oil, remained in use with minor changes and alterations. The earlier, as yet undeciphered, Linear A script used for the administrative records was replaced by Linear B script in Greek. Chamber tombs of mainland type appear for the first time around Knossos, at Sellopoulo and at other places and often contain burials of warriors with their weapons. After a time a great destruction followed, dated by the excavator Sir Arthur Evans to c.1400 BC, but in some recent studies perhaps to as late as 1250. After this catastrophe, the palace was not reconstructed. A few areas capable of repair continued to be used in different ways and the city surrounding the palace continued to thrive. Crete remained a distinctive but important part of the Mycenaean world. Later, during the Dark Age, Knossos was the most prosperous community in the whole of Greece, maintaining regular contact with Cyprus and Egypt.

Mycenae

The most important Mycenaean city on grounds of wealth and size, Mycenae was a fitting capital for Agamemnon. The citadel is situated on a rocky outcrop at the northern end of the Argive plain, guarding one of the main routes to the Corinthia. Around this was a community occupying some 32 hectares. The circuit of the walls (Fig. 4, p. 14) reached c. 1km. in length after a series of enlargements and had two principal entrances – the monumental Lion Gate and the North East Postern – as well as a small sallyport. An underground passage below the north wall gave access to a cistern cut around 1200 BC which was fed by a concealed aqueduct to provide a water supply in case of siege. Remains of the palace proper survive on the summit of the hill, although part has collapsed into the ravine below. The citadel is full of buildings of 13th-century date, of which the most imposing are the Granary beside the Lion Gate, the House of the Warrior Vase and the South House in the vicinity of Grave Circle A, together with the House of Columns at the northern end below the Palace.

Part of the western side of the citadel was used for a number of small shrines, including the Temple and the Room with the Fresco. A number of houses have been investigated outside the walls, including the House of the Oil Merchant, House of Sphinxes and House of Shields, all apparently rich dependencies of the Palace. A substantial road network linked Mycenae to other areas and traces of paved roads, bridges and culverts have been found in the area around the town.

The best known of the graves at Mycenae are the Shaft Graves sunk below Grave Circle A, where Schliemann found objects indicating astounding wealth with the burials. These were originally outside the walls and were only enclosed within them at a later date, while the earlier Grave Circle B about 150m. to the north west remains outside the circuit. Both circles belong to a large cemetery first used in the Middle Helladic period (2000-1650 BC) which extended along the north-western flank of the Acropolis hill. Nine tholos tombs have been found, including the immense Treasury of Atreus and the slightly smaller Tomb of Clytemnestra. Cemeteries containing well over 200 simpler rock-cut chamber tombs have been discovered around the town of Mycenae and help to delineate its extent.

Around 1200 BC, the Palace and many buildings were destroyed and only a reduced community remained to shelter within the walls. Eventually, by the end of the Mycenaean period, this had shrunk so much that graves were placed inside the circuit of the walls. Mycenae lost out in importance to Tiryns and to Argos, and never recovered its former position. In the Hellenistic period, c. 300 BC, the walls were repaired with squared, not Cyclopean, blocks to shelter a small community, prosperous enough to have its own theatre. The new buildings all over the citadel and around it which covered the Mycenaean remains can still be seen today, and will confuse the visitor without a good guide book.

Orchomenos

In legend the home of King Minyas, this site is located on a rocky spur at the north-western corner of the basin of Lake Copais, a shallow lake which has flooded more or less of the plain as its water rose or fell. Orchomenos was already important in the Early Bronze Age, c. 2500 BC, and there are traces of substantial Mycenaean buildings under the Classical and Hellenistic town. A variety of fragments of wall paintings from several areas provides further proof of the prosperity of its inhabitants.

The wealth of the ruler of Orchomenos is strikingly demonstrated by the ruins of a most elaborate tholos tomb, comparable to the Treasury of

Atreus at Mycenae. Although only the lower walls and the side chamber survive since the masonry was largely removed to build the Hellenistic theatre, the quality of the masonry and the superb carved decoration of the roof of the side chamber are outstanding.

The vast citadel known today as Gla, c.10km. away on the opposite side of the lake basin, was surely a dependency of the ruler of Orchomenos. Its Cyclopean walls, 2.6km. long, were constructed in the 13th century on what was once a rocky islet; but it is clear that much of the lake was drained by Mycenaean engineers at the same time to increase the cultivable area – an undertaking that was not attempted again until the present century. Within the circuit there were major buildings in palatial style, together with granaries and, possibly, stables. The site was destroyed by fire in the late 13th century BC and never reoccupied.

Pylos

The territory of Nestor, oldest and wisest of the Achaean heroes, was centred on sandy Pylos. There are at least three sites in the western Peloponnese which shared this name in the Classical period. However, the discovery of a Mycenaean palace at Ano Englianos near the gulf of Navarino makes it certain this Pylos was the principal city of Late Bronze Age Messenia, and the palace is now known as 'the Palace of Nestor'. From the beginning of the Mycenaean period rich burials in tumuli and tholoi in the vicinity suggest that it was one of the most prosperous areas of the Peloponnese – despite the lack of any natural resources other than agricultural ones. The palace is set, within sight of the sea, in a broken but fertile landscape on a ridge between two ravines which provides natural protection. An early version of the palace on a low hilltop was surrounded by a fortification wall, but the later building on the same site seems to have been unprotected. This is the best preserved of all the Mycenaean palace sites and its ground plan can be readily understood (Fig. 5, overleaf, and Chapter 7). It was surrounded by other buildings for storage and contained the largest group of Linear B tablets from Mainland Greece, of which most came from a room beside the entrance to the palace. A large town has been located around the palace hill but has not yet been fully explored.

This palace was also destroyed by a violent fire during the 13th century BC – possibly well before the destructions at Mycenae and other sites. A little activity took place here during the early part of the Dark Age, but the site had lost any importance.

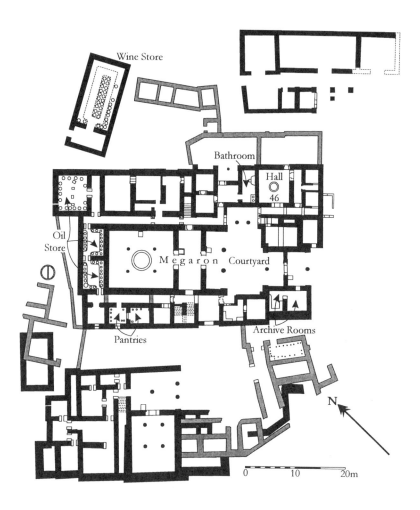

Fig. 5 The Palace of Nestor at Pylos in Messenia, c. 1225 BC.

Sparta

Geographically and as the legendary home of Menelaus and Helen, Sparta should have been one of the major Mycenaean cities. Situated in the fertile Eurotas valley, the area enjoyed many natural advantages. Although the remains are scanty, they tend to confirm the picture of a prosperous centre. There is nothing Mycenaean of note in the area of the Classical city, but a few kilometres to the south is a tholos tomb at Vapheio. This is one of the few tholoi where any finds remained for the archaeologist – notably gold cups decorated in repoussé with scenes of the capture of bulls. On the escarpment above the river to the east, close to a monument, the Menelaion, erected in honour of Helen and Menelaus in the archaic period, are the foundations of a substantial mansion, perhaps even an early palace. There is little to show what happened in the area during the Dark Age – except at the sanctuary of Amyklae where offerings were already being made in the Mycenaean period. Sparta was one of the principal communities of Dorians, who, according to tradition, arrived in the Peloponnese '80 years after the Trojan War'. Here, as elsewhere, there is little tangible sign of their coming, let alone anything to show when this event took place.

Thebes

None of the ancient cities of the heroic age had accumulated so many legends as seven-gated Thebes, seat of Cadmus and of Oedipus. It is not surprising that Cyclopean walls and major buildings of palatial quality, with fragments of fine wall-painting dating to the 14th and 13th centuries, have been found on the summit of a natural acropolis-like hill overlooking the fertile Boeotian plain. The 'seven gates' have not been found but the town has seven natural entrances where the gates of Classical Thebes were located. Different rooms near the so-called 'House of Cadmos' contained numerous ornaments of gold, lapis lazuli and ivory as well as bronze weapons, armour and horse bits. Even more remarkable was an 'antiquarian' collection of 42 antique Near Eastern cylinder seals, 39 of lapis lazuli and 3 of faience. Some were already a thousand years old when the building was destroyed by fire – perhaps evidence for the earliest museum. Numbers of Linear B tablets have been discovered in the same vicinity. Many tombs have been cut into the hills all around Thebes. Among these is a large rock-cut chamber tomb decorated with paintings of women on the doorjambs. It had two entrances which led the excavator to identify it with the tombs of the two sons of Oedipus, Eteocles and Polyneices. Interestingly, since ancient times this hill was believed to be a mound covering their tombs.

The palace buildings were destroyed towards the end of the 13th century BC and little is known of Thebes' Dark Age history.

Tiryns

Like Mycenae, this mighty citadel, ruled by Diomedes, survived the ages to astonish with the height and thickness of its walls. Originally it was a coastal town, on the edge of the Argolid plain, perhaps with a harbour for Mycenae, since the coastline has advanced several hundred metres since the Bronze Age. The site was already important in the Early Bronze Age (c. 2500 BC) and the Mycenaean citadel was built on a small outcrop of limestone and divided into three sections. The upper part of the citadel contained the palace, the lower part, buildings which probably served palace officials. The main entrance was reached up a sloping ramp on the east and through a narrow passage flanked with high walls and barred with a stout wooden gate. A narrow stair in the thickness of the wall provided an exit via a small sally-port on the west side. Two passages below the walls of the lower citadel were cut around 1200 BC to provide protected access to water. The thickness of the walls was used everywhere to provide extra space – perhaps for storage, notably in the two sets of galleries at the southern end (Fig. 20, p. 59). The palace is remarkable for the series of courtyards through which entrance was gained and for the carved stone base for a throne found in the principal room of the *megaron* (the king's hall). Fragments of wall-paintings, including a scene of bull-leaping, from below the floor indicate the presence of an even earlier palace. A large settlement is known outside the walls but little has yet been explored. Two tholos tombs and a series of chamber tombs have been discovered cut into the hills to the east. A few kilometres away to the east is a massive earth dam which was created to block a torrent bed and divert the stream away from the citadel – another example of the skill and enterprise of Mycenaean engineers.

With the destructions of 1200 BC, Tiryns was possibly the only Mycenaean site to retain some of its palatial character. The megaron itself was rebuilt on a smaller scale and the town was perhaps larger than it had ever been before. Cemeteries of 11th- and 10th-century BC date show that it remained a site of importance well into the Dark Age.

Troy

The goal of the Achaean expedition, the city to which Paris had taken the fair Helen, had existed in a strategic position close to the mouth of the Dardanelles in NW Anatolia since the beginning of the Bronze Age (c. 3500 BC). Here it controlled the trade routes from the Aegean to the Black Sea or from western Anatolia to Europe and, with few local natural resources, became extraordinarily wealthy. The treasure that Schliemann found in Troy II, and mistakenly thought was Priam's, belonged to the Early Bronze Age. The massive fortifications were repeatedly renewed and enlarged. By the Late Bronze Age (Troy VI) the inner citadel occupied an area of 2 hectares with walls well over 7m. high. Some buildings survive inside these walls but most had been removed by the levelling carried out in the Hellenistic and Roman periods. Outside the citadel and protected by a defensive ditch was a large town whose extent is still being explored. Pottery and other remains show that this was an Anatolian site, but Mycenaean pottery is quite frequent and demonstrates the normally 'friendly' relations with the Mycenaean cities of southern Greece. This period was brought to an end by earthquake in the 13th century, and subsequently less impressive buildings were constructed within the citadel walls (Troy VIIa) which were later destroyed by fire. One of these may well be the Troy of the epic siege but opinions differ as to which.

Troy continued to be occupied throughout the Dark Age and, like Mycenae, its walls towered above the plain for many centuries. The Classical Greeks and the Romans after them had no doubt that this was the Troy of legend. It was only the Roman building programme which finally hid them from view and gave rise to the long debate about its location and even its very existence.

Fig. 6 Seal impression on clay from Chania, Crete, ht 3cm, c. 1500 BC. A man holding a spear stands proudly on the parapet of a many-storeyed town with two gates by the sea.

Fig. 7 Grave Circle A at Mycenae, c. 1880 AD, from North. The double ring of stones was placed in this position, in the 13th century BC, long after the last burial.

Chapter 4
Tombs and burial practices

Much of what is known about the Mycenaeans comes from their tombs. The form of the tomb can indicate the position of the deceased in society, while the widespread practice of one family using the same tomb generation after generation points to the essential stability of their community. The offerings made in the tomb – whether intended for use by the dead in the next world or to display the wealth of the living – illustrate the burial customs of the time as well as showing the status of the dead person, but also reveal the wide range of raw materials available and the skills of Mycenaean craftsmen (Chapter 5). Some elaborate tombs required much labour and considerable expertise for their construction. Others show such a profusion of rich offerings that it is assumed that they were for the leading members of society, the numerous 'kings' and 'princes' of the Homeric epic – though caution is needed in using these terms.

Tomb types

Before the Mycenaean period most burials were individual, in tombs which were simple, shallow pits cut in the ground, or lined and covered with slabs of rock (*cist graves*). These tombs are found in isolation or in small groups rather than in large cemeteries, and are usually too short to allow a fully extended burial. The body was therefore curled on the side in a contracted position, often on a prepared floor of river pebbles. Late in the Middle Bronze Age (c. 1700 BC), some tombs, especially wealthier ones, start to be grouped under a mound of earth – a *tumulus* – suggesting family members or retainers of a local chieftain. This practice is particularly common in Messenia. With the first burial, the body was often laid on the surface of the ground and covered with stones before the tumulus was raised over it. Later burials, cut through the mound, might be on the original surface, while others were in pits or cists, or placed in huge jars (*pithoi*). The mound was intended to be seen from a distance and was often marked in addition by a large stone or *stele*.

The earlier of the Grave Circles at Mycenae, that called B because it was found later, seems to illustrate the same concept. Although there is

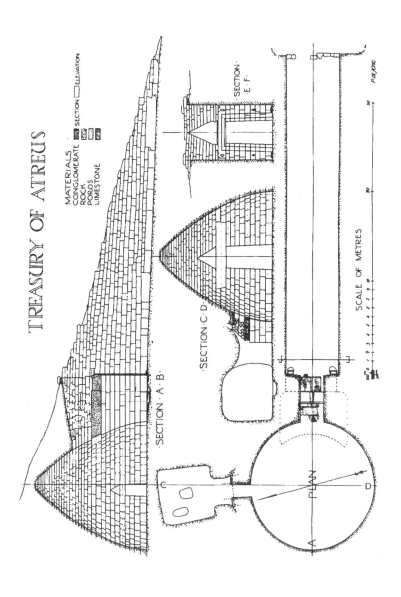

Fig. 8 Treasury of Atreus at Mycenae c. 1350 BC.

little evidence for a mound covering the 24 graves, they were enclosed at some point with a low wall of rough stones, marking out a specific group from the other tombs scattered over the north-western slope of the Mycenae citadel. The first graves in the circle date to the Middle Bronze Age and are no different from other cist and pit graves. The burials are still contracted and the offerings are no richer than those elsewhere. Later, wealthier burials were placed in larger, deeper pits, the first true *shaft graves*. These were cut up to two and a half metres into the rock and the largest measures 3.9 × 3.4m. A chamber was created at the base of the shaft, either by leaving a rock ledge to support the beams of a roof, by building a secondary wall to support them or by using wooden posts. The burial could now be fully extended and in some cases there was room for several bodies on the tomb floor – though it is not always clear whether these were contemporary or successive. After the burial the roof was put in place, the shaft filled with earth and the grave marked with a plain or decorated stone stele, up to 2m. in height.

The well-preserved skulls from these tombs have provided a remarkable opportunity to visualise these Mycenaean leaders – in the reconstruction of their features by Richard Neave and John Prag (Fig. 10, p. 31).

At the beginning of the Mycenaean period a new area was chosen for the richest graves, before Circle B went out of use. Further to the south along the west flank of the citadel hill, (and later included within the citadel wall when it was extended), is the group of tombs, known as Grave Circle A, found by Schliemann (Fig. 7, p. 24), which continues the same burial practices. Here there is no evidence for the original boundary wall, if any, since the present circle is the product of a landscaping programme during the 13th century BC. The six large shafts thus enclosed were cut in the soft limestone which forms the bedrock in this area. A seventh similar grave remained outside the later circle. The shafts were even deeper, up to 4m., and larger than those in Circle B. Although Schliemann's excavation techniques were relatively primitive, it is clear that these graves were reopened and disturbed on several occasions to make additional burials since the fill of the shafts contained scraps of gold ornament from earlier ones. The wealth of gold and imported materials found in these graves shows the very high status of their occupants – already indicated by the establishment of a separate burial precinct.

Other true shaft graves, with a chamber at their base, rather than just a deep pit, are rare.

Tumuli continued in use into the Mycenaean period and in some cases – as at Marathon – were provided with stone-built burial chambers. A second tumulus at Marathon carried this idea a stage further with a built central chamber and a 'passage' leading almost to the edge of the mound. From here it is but a small step to the concept of the monumental tholos tomb, so characteristic of Mycenaean 'princely' burials from the 15th century BC on (Chapter 7). The earliest tholoi, as well as the earliest tumuli, seem to have been constructed in Messenia. They were usually set on flat ground, as at Pylos, with a circular stone-built chamber and a passage (*dromos*) leading up to it. The whole was then covered with a mound of earth to support the rough masonry and protect it. Later tombs were sited on sloping hillsides so that the passage, which now led to a cylindrical shaft, could be cut into it. The masonry of the tomb was built into the shaft and gradually closed to a vault using the *corbelling* technique, while the top of the chamber rose above ground level and was covered with earth forming a visible tumulus. Great skill and much labour was needed for the construction of these tholos tombs and they must be seen as the burial places of persons of high rank, perhaps kings or princes, constructed in advance during their lifetimes.

While the wealthy rulers could afford such considerable expense, the next social level of the Mycenaean population was content with simpler rock-cut tombs wherever the natural geology allowed. These chamber tombs appear soon after the first tholoi, cut in the same way into a sloping hillside with a dromos but using the rock to form the walls and roof of a square or rounded chamber. These were family graves, perhaps prepared in advance in cemeteries which might contain dozens of tombs. What proportion of the Mycenaean population received burial in this kind of tomb is uncertain. Although scores of tombs and hundreds of burials are known there still seems to be a 'missing' element, perhaps of those too poor or insignificant to receive burial at all.

While tholoi were rarely built after the end of the 14th century BC, chamber tombs were constructed and reused throughout the Mycenaean period and in a number of cases persisted in use into the succeeding Iron Age. Some of the 12th-century BC tombs contain examples of a new funeral rite – cremation – but the numbers involved are still very small and they may represent exceptional circumstances rather than imported ideas or immigrant populations. Examples are known from most parts of Greece from Elis in the west to Mycenae in the Argolid and Perati in Attica in the east. Only with the advent of the Iron Age, and then only in some centres such as Knossos on Crete, Euboea and Attica, is cremation adopted as the predominant rite.

With the decline of Mycenaean prosperity and increasing instability towards the end of the 12th century BC, an old burial practice – the use of single pit or cist graves – becomes popular once again as graves were prepared for the immediate need rather than planned for future generations. In some places, notably on the island of Salamis and at the Kerameikos in Athens, or Lefkandi in Euboea, new cemetery areas were brought into use which in some cases continued to receive burials past the end of the Mycenaean period.

Burial customs

It is rare to find a Mycenaean tomb which did not have any offerings or *grave-goods*, although many had been robbed, either soon after the burial had taken place or in consequence of the illicit trade in antiquities. Those objects in the grave which survive the tomb robbers or natural decay (for, like the flesh, clothing and items of wood or leather have long since vanished) provide some idea of the wealth or status of the deceased, if they can be associated with an individual burial. For most of the Mycenaean period, however, since tombs were reused over tens if not hundreds of years, it is often impossible to decide which objects belong with which skeleton. Moreover, since the earlier remains were treated with scant respect, the tombs often contain heaps of bones and offerings pushed to one side and only a single skeleton from the latest interment with its bones in position. Valuable objects may well have been removed when later burials took place. Few skeletons are well enough preserved to permit their sex to be identified (and fewer of these have actually been studied), so that the presence of weapons or jewellery is often used to distinguish between male and female burials.

There are a few hints about the funeral ritual. That the body was clothed and adorned can be deduced from the position of jewellery at the neck or wrists, or weapons at the side. Other objects were placed around the body – or even under it in some cases, showing that it was laid on a bier or stretcher. The use of a clay *larnax* or burial chest, as at Tanagra in Boeotia where they are painted with scenes of mourning, is elsewhere very rare. Following the funeral rites at the tomb, the entrance was closed – with a door in the case of the great tholoi or a blocking wall of rough stones in the case of the chamber tombs, and a last 'toast' drunk or a last libation poured by the mourners. Tall stemmed drinking cups (*kylikes*) which were sometimes coated with tin, presumably to suggest silver vessels, were used for this final 'toast' and are regularly found smashed on the floor of the entrance passage.

Grave- goods

The majority of the objects placed in the grave at the time of burial are

Fig. 9 Gold masks from Grave Circle A as found by Schliemann, c. 1550 BC.
a) Grave IV, ht 30.3cm; b) Grave V, ht 26cm. (These look more life-like if you curve
the page!)

a

Fig. 10 Two princes from Grave Γ in Circle B at Mycenae, reconstructed from the skulls by Richard Neave and John Prag.

a) died after an operation to trepan his skull.

b) had a face mask of electrum.

(Photographs courtesy The Manchester Museum and Unit of Art in Medicine, University of Manchester.)

b

pottery vessels, mostly jars or jugs which must have contained liquid or semi-liquid offerings such as oil or wine, ointment, perfume or honey. Bronze weapons – sword and spear – and knives or jewellery in the form of pendants and necklaces are the commonest additional offerings, though occasionally 'tools of the trade' are found such as lead net-weights from Perati in Attica. In the earlier Mycenaean period, large bronze vessels are quite frequent and precious metal drinking vessels surprisingly common. Valuable items like ivory boxes and combs, ivory-handled bronze mirrors or stone vases are rarer while sheet-gold body ornament is almost entirely restricted to the Shaft Graves at Mycenae. Among the most valuable of all offerings was a pair of horses, slaughtered at the time of the funeral, as found at Marathon or Dendra. Clay figurines and models were sometimes placed in the grave.

The offerings would all be suitable for use in an afterlife, but it cannot be deduced (as it can for the Egyptian civilization) that this was a positive belief. Many items could simply be demonstrations of wealth and status, ostentatiously displayed in the funeral procession and in the tomb with the corpse. The 'expense' of burying objects of gold and silver, horses, or quantities of bronze, suggests that the living still had plenty for their own use. When, as at the very end of the Mycenaean period, grave-goods become scarce, it is a further indication of economic decline.

The Shaft Graves at Mycenae

The contents of the Shaft Graves, as an assemblage, remain without parallel. The wealth of objects illustrate the availability of precious raw materials, the range and skill of the craftsmen and the resources of those who were buried. When trying to understand what was found in each grave, it should be noted that Schliemann's numbering of the graves is no longer used today:

Schliemann's number	Current number
1	V
2	I
3	III
4	IV
5	II
Stamatakis' grave	VI

Of the two sets of graves, the later ones discovered by Schliemann below Circle A are the richest. Together they contained about 14kg. of sheet-gold fashioned into face masks reproducing the features of the dead (Fig. 9, p. 30), richly decorated diadems (Fig. 12, p. 38) and breast coverings, elaborate necklaces, showy earrings, and hosts of rosettes and other ornaments originally stitched or glued to the funeral shrouds. Drinking cups and jars of gold and silver accompanied the men, women and children buried in the graves. The so-called Cup of Nestor – with handles on either side and a pair of doves at the top of the handles looking inwards – is perhaps the most famous of these. It resembles in some ways, although not in size, the description of the *depas amphikypellon* used by Nestor (*Iliad* Book XI, 632). Many gold cups were fluted or ribbed to give strength to the soft metal of their sides. Four gold goblets with dogs' heads on the handles were found in the vicinity of the Shaft Graves and may originally have belonged to a disturbed grave.

Other gold objects included a cylindrical box (*pyxis*), an amphora and a pouring vessel of the type known as a *rhyton* fashioned in the form of a lion's head. Silver vessels included goblets, a jug and two relief-decorated vases – the 'Battle Krater' and the 'Siege Rhyton' – illustrating furious combat. Other *rhyta* were fashioned from silver in the form of a stag, or the head of a bull with golden horns. Giant vessels of bronze and lead were also discovered in several graves.

There were dozens of long bronze rapiers and heavy spears (see Chapter 8), together with six short daggers inlaid with gold, silver and a kind of black enamel (known as *niello*) to depict scenes of battle or hunting (Fig. 12), a river scene with leopards stalking birds, or lions attacking deer. These daggers are among the finest products made by Aegean craftsmen, showing extraordinary levels of delicacy and skill, together with a fine sense of composition.

Imported materials included amber beads from northern Europe, some in the form of the *spacer beads* also known from the Wessex culture of southern England; ostrich eggs from North Africa transformed into vessels in the Aegean; ivory from Egypt or Syria carved into a wide variety of objects; Cretan stone vases; lapis lazuli from Afghanistan made into beads and inlays, as well as beads and other objects of *faience*. In Grave Circle A, at least, pottery vessels were less common than items of precious materials, but they enable the burials to be dated.

Grave Circle B, found in 1951, was earlier and less opulent. One of the dead had a face mask of *electrum* (a natural mixture of gold and silver), and there were many items of jewellery, including five long pins with heads of hard rock crystal, and body ornaments of gold. Numerous weapons were also found, together with vessels of gold and silver. Of particular note are a rock crystal bowl in the form of a duck and a minute amethyst seal-stone showing the head of a bearded man. Pottery was much more frequent in these graves and included many examples of *matt-painted* Middle Helladic types as well as some of the earliest pottery in the lustrous Mycenaean technique.

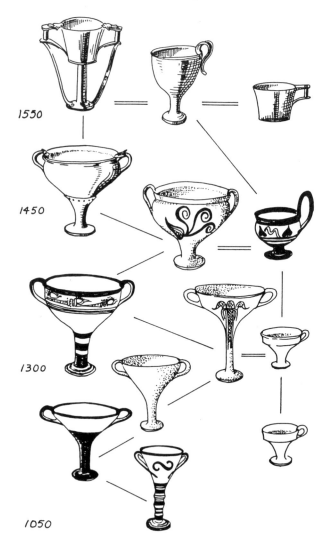

Fig. 11 The development of drinking vessels – goblets and kylikes – in metal and pottery, 1550 - 1050 BC.

Chapter 5
Materials and technology

The contents of graves, like those described in the previous chapter, provide a wealth of information about the range of materials available in the Mycenaean world, the skills and technologies used to work them and the enormous variety of their products. Pottery, metalwork, the carving of stone and ivory as well as the use of glass all attest their technical expertise and artistic achievement. For examples of other skills such as textile production, wood carving, or the manufacture of perfume, the evidence is largely and necessarily indirect. Much must be deduced from wall-paintings and the Linear B tablets.

Pottery

In the Mycenaean period, pottery for storage, cooking or the table, or for transport of large or small amounts of liquids, was manufactured in quantity in all parts of Southern and Central Greece. The clay selected was of good quality and matched to the function of the intended vessel, shaped on the potter's wheel and evenly fired at high temperature to produce a durable product. The shapes were remarkably standardised and included drinking vessels in the form of goblets, cups, mugs or tall-stemmed kylikes, vessels for the table such as the large mixing bowls (*kraters*), and smaller, deep or shallow bowls. Flat plates, however, are unknown. Storage containers ranged from the large pithoi, 1.5m. or more high, to narrow necked *amphorae* of different sizes or the distinctive Mycenaean *stirrup jar* with an offset spout for easy control when pouring (Fig. 30, p. 101). Large stirrup jars were used for transport of oil while smaller, often elaborately decorated, examples contained the finished product, presumably perfumed oil, for use in life or as an offering in a grave. Other shapes included small wide-mouthed jars, with three handles used for securing a cover, which could have held an ointment or paste and would not spill readily; feeding bottles for children; and jugs in a wide range of shapes and sizes. Pottery rhyta – the name given to the funnel-like vessels for measuring or ritual pouring – were also made in more elaborate shapes, such as animal heads, perhaps imitating examples in precious metals like those from the Shaft Graves. Tripod-legged cooking pots and rectangular grill stands were made in a coarse, specially prepared clay better able to stand the heat of the cooking hearth. Clay was also used for large vats and *larnakes* (burial caskets) or even large bath tubs.

Fortunately for the archaeologist, production of this wheelmade pottery in many areas was so large and so standardised that a semi-industrial scale of manufacture may reasonably be conjectured. The rapid changes in fashion spread quickly throughout the Mycenaean world. For this reason the Swedish scholar Arne Furumark was able to compile a pattern book showing how shapes and motifs changed over time, in a closely dated sequence. Thus individual pots may be dated accurately in this sequence of development.

The patterns were applied to Mycenaean pottery before firing with an iron-rich clay slip which fired to a glossy red or black depending on the kiln atmosphere. Earlier Middle Helladic matt-painted pottery used a manganese-rich slip which fired to a dull purple red, little affected by kiln temperature or atmosphere. Mycenaean decoration, on the whole, is built up in parallel zones with the lower body of most vessels painted with simple banding or, in the later periods, solid colour. The motifs used are frequently so stylised that the original design can only be tracked down with difficulty. Early motifs include double axes, leaves, bold spirals and even a kind of stippling or sponging imitating eggshell. Spirals remain popular, while stylised flowers and *whorl-shells* are common in the palatial period together with *panelled* patterns using vertical lines and zigzags. Later designs are often painted with a thinner brush and can be very detailed. Figured decoration also flourished during the palatial period, when favourite themes on the large kraters are chariot scenes or bulls. These were particularly popular in Cyprus, and part of the output of the production centres in the Argolid may have been specifically for export to that island. Figured scenes reappear after the destructions of 1200 BC, but are relatively rare. They include the famous 'Warrior Vase' found by Schliemann, an exceptionally large krater decorated with a file of soldiers marching out to battle on either side (cf. Fig. 40, p. 135). After these destructions, linear decoration predominates and the use of patterns is much reduced. This may be the result of a greater economy of effort in the period of economic decline after the disappearance of the palaces.

A combination of wheelmade and handmade techniques were used for a wide variety of clay figures and models of different sizes ranging from human figures to animals or chariot groups, often thought to have a religious function (see Chapter 11). Notable, but unusual, examples are the 'ugly' figures and coiled snakes from the Temple at Mycenae

(Fig. 36, p. 117), the 'Lady of Phylakopi' and the wheelmade cow figures from a 12th-century BC shrine in the island of Melos. Small female figurines in the shape of the Greek letters *phi, psi* and *tau* and small horned bovids are the most common.

Metalwork

By the Mycenaean period the only workable mineral deposits in southern Greece were probably those in eastern Attica at Laurion which produced copper and silver-bearing lead. In Macedonia there were rich sources of copper and gold. Despite the lack of mineral resources in most of Greece, Mycenaean society used metal in astonishing quantities and the search for this was one of the factors underlying the extensive pattern of trade (see Chapter 10).

Gold was freely available and used regularly for vessels, jewellery and finger rings, as well as the more exotic items in the Shaft Graves (Chapter 4). Gold seal rings are engraved with elaborate scenes which often seem to have some cult symbolism: one of the best known examples is the 'Great Goddess' ring (Fig. 33, p. 110), part of a hoard of valuable objects found near Grave Circle A. It shows a seated woman, perhaps a goddess or priestess, holding poppy heads in her hands, and approached by women holding flowers. The same skill and delicacy of engraving on a small scale is seen in the 'Daemon' ring from the Tiryns Treasure, depicting upright scaly-backed creatures carrying rhyta to make offerings to a seated figure Fig. 32, p. 108). Other rings, including some with hunting scenes, have been found in early burials in chamber tombs at many sites. That these were treasured items is shown by the discovery of well-worn examples, (on which the decoration is hardly preserved), in later contexts – as in 12th-century BC graves at Perati in Eastern Attica. The subject matter and 'engraving' technique has much in common with the stone sealstones (see p. 43).

The techniques of **granulation** and **cloisonné** (Fig. 12, overleaf) were used by goldsmiths to produce objects of astonishing delicacy. Cloisonné involved soldering a pattern of fine wire on to a base plate such as a ring or sword hilt and setting it with inlays of stone or glass. Sword and dagger hilts could be elaborately decorated with inlays of lapis lazuli and crystal. Granulation used precisely placed droplets of gold to decorate beads, rings and other objects such as a frog from Pylos and a wild goat from Thebes. Both techniques require great skill and a very precise control of temperature.

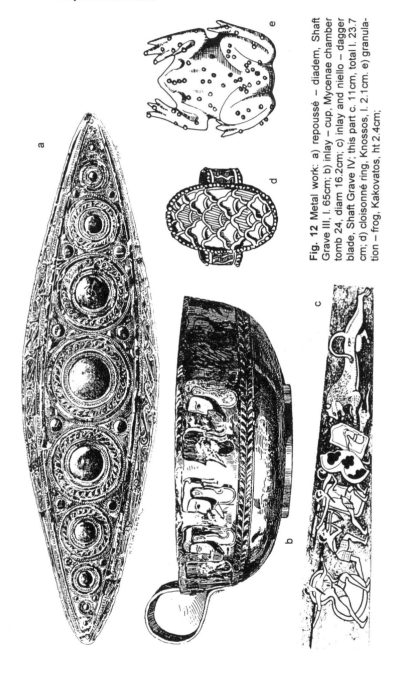

Fig. 12 Metal work: a) repoussé – diadem, Shaft Grave III, l. 65cm; b) inlay – cup, Mycenae chamber tomb 24, diam 16.2cm; c) inlay and niello – dagger blade, Shaft Grave IV; this part c. 11cm, total l. 23.7 cm; d) cloisonné ring, Knossos, l. 2.1cm. e) granulation – frog, Kakovatos, ht 2.4cm;

The technique of metal **inlay** was frequently used to great effect. Gold was inlaid into the blades of bronze swords. Gold, silver and black enamel (compounds of copper, and copper and silver sulphides frequently referred to as *niello*), were inlaid into the blades of daggers to depict a lion hunt, geometric spiral ornaments or leopards and marine life. The bowls of drinking cups or goblets were favoured with plant motifs – or even human heads in profile (Fig. 12). The technique was also used in the Near East – notably for a silver cup with bulls' heads from Enkomi in Cyprus – and in Crete as well as mainland Greece.

The Linear B tablets from Pylos include a number of records of contributions of gold from important local officials totalling more than 5kg. – perhaps a special levy to help 'finance' the war effort (Chapter 8). Others seem to describe gold vessels or 'golden' furniture, perhaps covered with gold foil or inlaid. A single tablet from Pylos lists thirteen gold cups, some plain, some decorated. One from Knossos shows a drawing of a bull's head vessel, made from gold.

Repoussé – the technique of hammering up an elaborate pattern from the inside of gold and silver objects (Fig. 12) – can be seen in a number of pieces such as gold cups decorated with scenes of bull hunting from the Vapheio tholos near Sparta, a gold lion's head from the Shaft Graves and a gold cup decorated with sea creatures from Dendra in the Argolid. Two silver vessels from Mycenae are decorated with elaborate scenes of warfare.

Silver was apparently much rarer (though it does not survive well) and used principally for vessels, pins and inlays. **Electrum** has been noted from time to time, but without more analyses of composition it is difficult to know how widespread its use was. **Lead** was apparently very common – large quantities of *galena* (lead ore) were smelted at Laurion in the hope of extracting the silver, but only some of the metal produced would have been suitable for *cupellation*, the technique used to extract worthwhile amounts of silver. Cupellation is carried out by heating a small quantity of silver-bearing lead until molten and then passing a strong current of air over the surface with a blowpipe or similar tool. The lead oxidises in preference to the silver to form *litharge* which is then repeatedly skimmed off the surface to leave a higher and higher concentration of silver. Lead was also used for objects as diverse as vessels and fishing-net weights but most regularly for clamps for mending pottery – often of purely domestic character – which gives some idea of the relative value of the pottery. Neither silver nor lead receive much mention in the Linear B record from Pylos, perhaps because one was rare and the other commonplace.

Copper and **bronze** (an alloy of copper and tin in the proportion 9:1) were the predominant metals in use but they cannot be distinguished without chemical analysis and the term *bronze* is generally used indiscriminately. Copper is more flexible and thus suitable for objects requiring sheet metal – vessels, armour etc – while bronze with its lower melting point is easier to cast into complex shapes – such as swords and spears, axes, handle fittings or polished mirrors. It is both harder and more brittle. Copper was obtained from Laurion, Cyprus and Sardinia while the origin of the tin remains uncertain. There are no sources known in the Aegean, and the Mycenaean search for it provided another spur to long-range trade. Since metal can be so readily recycled, much bronze has vanished from view, especially the everyday objects which were not often placed in graves.

Scraps of melted bronze from the palace destructions, suggest that wooden doors and other features were embellished with bronze bindings, fittings and nails. The hinge posts of some doors were protected against wear with heavy bronze covers, set into sockets in the stone lintels and thresholds. Bronze swords and spears, daggers, knives and cleavers are often found in graves. Other military equipment included shield and chariot fittings as well as armour (Chapter 8). Domestic items include cups, jugs, amphorae, braziers, cauldrons, frying pans, ladles and lamps etc. Although bronze was used for such personal items as mirrors, tweezers and razors, jewellery is only found in the form of *fibulae* (brooches), long pins, bracelets and finger rings which became common in the period of economic decline at the end of the Mycenaean period. Many tools such as axes, chisels, hammers, saws, drill bits and even anvils were certainly made of bronze, but rarely placed in graves. The same is true of agricultural implements such as picks and broad-bladed hoes, sickles and folding pruning-knives. The largest collection of these, as well as other tools and scrap metal for re-working, was found in the Gelidonya wreck off the south coast of Turkey. A wide variety of other bronze items include horse bits, fishhooks, octopus spears, scale pans and needles, to name but a few. (See Chapter 10 for more details of the copper trade and the cargoes of this and the Kaş wreck).

A large group of documents at Pylos provides us with an astonishing picture of the number of bronzesmiths working for the palace. Even though the record is incomplete, nearly 300 smiths are mentioned working at different centres, some in groups of up to 26 individuals. Curiously, none has a very large ration of bronze: between 3 and 4kg. seems to be the normal amount. The maximum received was 12kg. and about one third of their number had no allocation. A unique tablet requests local officials to collect metal for the manufacture of weapons. A series from Knossos deals with 60 of the ingots in which the metal was traded, with a total weight of about 1.5 tonnes.

Iron, although known to the Mycenaeans, was exceptionally rare until the 12th century (Chapter 12).

Carving

Examples of Mycenaean **ivory carving** illustrate the considerable levels of skill attained in working a wide variety of materials. Little of wood survives: an important exception is a wooden box from the Grave Circle A with decorative gold plates set around it. Imported ivory from elephant and hippopotamus was a more valuable, and indeed durable, material used for a wide range of functions. It was used for parts of furniture, such as a pair of legs found at Thebes, or perhaps even complete chairs like one found in an 8th-century BC grave at Salamis on Cyprus. It can be found on the hilt plates of weapons or used for their pommels, and as intricately carved handles for bronze mirrors or combs. Segments of elephant tusks form the bodies of cylindrical boxes (*pyxides*). A fine example from Thebes has opposing pairs of sphinxes (Fig. 13, overleaf). Ivory inlays depicting a vast range of subjects – sphinxes, dolphins, shields, shells or columns – decorated furniture and chests. Ivory pieces carved in the round, such as the couchant lion and the youth's head from the Room with the Fresco at Mycenae (see Frontispiece, p. x), are much rarer but carved with supreme skill. Perhaps the finest example of this is the exquisitely carved 'Ivory Trio' from the acropolis at Mycenae, which depicts a pair of women and a small child (Fig. 24, p. 79).

The tablets record furniture including tables, chairs and footstools. Some of these were decorated with inlays of gold, ivory, wood and *kyanos* (see *faience* below) with scenes including men, horses, octopuses and birds.

Stone carving of small objects never became as common in mainland Greece as in Crete, perhaps because there were fewer available soft stones. Most of the earlier examples of stone vases, such as those from the Shaft Graves, are usually said to be of Cretan manufacture. By the Mycenaean Palatial period there were certainly mainland workshops which produced the fine vases found in the House of Shields at Mycenae. Hard basalt *mortars*, shaped in the form of a shallow bowl with three stumpy legs, which were used for grinding cereals, have been found at many sites. The large *stelai*, which once marked the position of the graves in the two Grave Circles at Mycenae, were carved with varying

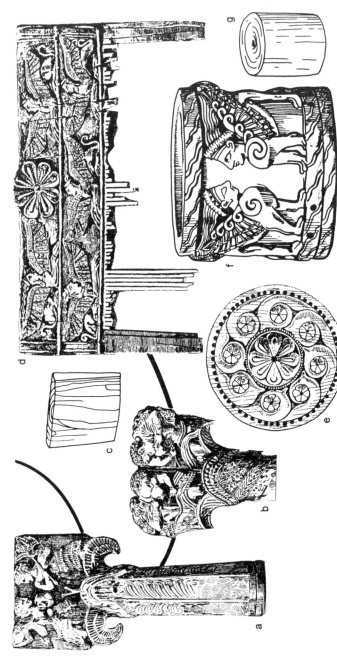

Fig. 13 Carved ivory: mirror handles, Chamber Tomb 55, Mycenae; a) ht 17cm; Clytemnestra Tholos, Mycenae; b) width 7.5cm; c) blank for comb, Mycenae.

d) comb, Spata, Attica, l. 14.4cm; e) pyxis lid, Mycenae, diam 6cm; f) pyxis from Thebes, ht 4.8cm; g) pyxis blank, Kaş wreck.

skill with patterns of spirals or hunting scenes. The superb decoration of the Lion Gate and the facade of the Treasury of Atreus at Mycenae (Fig. 17, p. 54), as well as the ceiling of the side chamber of the Orchomenos tholos (Fig. 18, p. 56) and the throne base at Tiryns, illustrate the time and labour devoted to monumental buildings.

Beads of native stones include rock crystal, carnelian, agate, sardonyx, steatite and amethyst; amber and lapis lazuli were imported. Bronze pins from both Grave Circles have carved rock crystal heads. *Sealstones*, usually small lentil-shaped beads with delicately carved scenes, have been found at many sites. The scenes are extraordinarily varied, depicting single animals such as bulls or deer, animals with young, lions in combat with bulls, or figures which may represent humans or divinities. They are not as common as in Crete, usually thought to be the principal centre of manufacture, and become rarer following the destruction of the Cretan palaces. Just as in Crete, they could be used to identify property or guarantee the contents of a jar or container, by single or multiple impressions on the clay *sealing* attached to it. Seal impressions of this kind were found on the clay stoppers on the jars in the House of the Oil Merchant at Mycenae (Fig. 30, p. 101) or associated with the Linear B records at Pylos. These sealstones were often included in a necklace or bracelet and the scene on them may have been supposed to act as a kind of *talisman* (magic charm) to protect the wearer.

Glass and faience

The technique of **faience** production – the firing of a coloured glaze on the surface of an unvitrified soft core – is generally thought to be Egyptian in origin. True **glass** (often described in this period as *glass paste*), which has a uniform composition from surface to core, may also originate in this region. The raw materials, silica sand and potash, are widely available. Malleable at quite low temperatures, this glass can readily be moulded and Mycenaean craftsmen used the technique frequently for the production of ornamental beads or for inlays. Intricately cut stone moulds for making glass or gold beads and pendants have been found at Mycenae (Fig. 14, overleaf) and other sites, while mention is made in a number of Linear B tablets of *kyanos* workers, presumed to be glass-makers. The blue colour of many beads, produced by copper minerals, may well have served as a cheaper substitute for the rare lapis lazuli from Afghanistan. The discovery of ingots of three different colours of glass as part of the cargo of the late 14th-century Kaş wreck, found off the south coast of Turkey, suggest that the raw material was, in some cases, produced in the Near East and traded widely. Fine decorated vessels such as the faience vase fragments from Mycenae with lotus buds (Fig. 14a), a warrior's head and a lion and griffin may have been imported.

a

Piet de Jong.

Fig. 14 a) Faience goblet from House of Shields, Mycenae, ht 12.5cm, c. 1250 BC; b) jewellery mould from area of Cult Centre at Mycenae, l. 10.5cm, late 13th century BC; c) glass jewellery of the kind made in mould (b), as found at many Mycenaean sites.

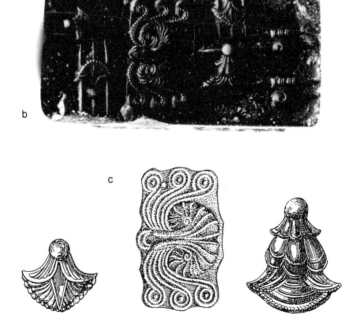

b

c

Chapter 6
Economy and society

The Linear B archives

No literature or historical accounts survive from the Mycenaean period – unless the Homeric epics are regarded as Bronze Age poetry – but the chance preservation of a large number of clay tablets inscribed with administrative records provides an exciting extra dimension to the understanding of Mycenaean civilization, unparalleled in prehistoric Europe. There are still only two sites where large numbers of these tablets have been discovered – Knossos in Crete (over 7000 fragments) and the Palace of Nestor at Pylos (about 1200 fragments) – but examples come from most of the major centres: Mycenae and Tiryns in mainland Greece and Chania in Western Crete. Another group has been found at Thebes. The same form of writing, but painted, was also used to mark some pottery transport jars before firing to denote their origin or contents.

The language of the tablets was identified by Michael Ventris as an early form of Greek in 1952, although it took some time before everyone accepted this decipherment. Like all the contemporary Near Eastern scripts it was written in *syllabic* form, using over a hundred different signs to convey the range of sounds used, each one a combination of consonant and vowel. There are similarities with the distinctive dialect of the Homeric epics but its closest descendant was the dialect of Arcadia in the heart of the Peloponnese. Like Classical Greek, the nouns and verbs are inflected on standard stems and many words and proper names are immediately recognisable. Separate symbols known as *ideograms* depict animals such as rams and pigs, objects like jars or swords or commodities including wheat and cloth (Fig. 15, overleaf). Sometimes the written word is amplified by an ideogram on the same line. This system allowed those less literate than the Mycenaean scribes to understand the record and certainly helps the modern student in decipherment. Numerals and signs for wet and dry weights and measures complete the repertoire of Linear B script. Examples of different 'handwriting' can be identified, showing that there were at least thirty scribes at Pylos and over sixty at Knossos.

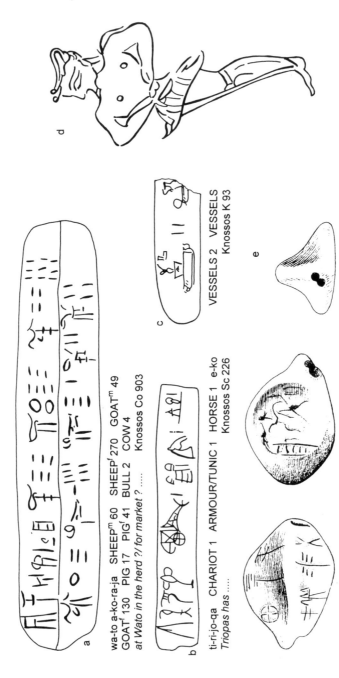

wa-to a-ko-ra-ja   SHEEP^m 60   SHEEP^f 270   GOAT^m 49
GOAT^f 130   PIG 17   PIG^f 41   BULL 2   COW 4
at Wato in the herd ?/ for market ? ......   Knossos Co 903

ti-ri-jo-qa   CHARIOT 1   ARMOUR/TUNIC 1   HORSE 1   e-ko
Triopas has .....   Knossos Sc 226

VESSELS 2   VESSELS
Knossos K 93

Fig. 15 a-c) Linear B leaf tablets from Knossos, l. 18, 11, 6cm; d) graffito on reverse of tablet and (e) inscribed sealing, from House of Sphinxes, Mycenae, l. 2.8cm, c. 1250 BC, reading ka-na-to and pa-ke-te-re. One of seven labels probably attached to vessels and found with a page tablet bearing an inventory of them.

At the time a transaction took place – the receipt or issue of a commodity, or an inventory of a storeroom, for example – the scribe would record the details on a fresh tablet of soft damp clay with a thin pointed tool. These tablets were then left to dry to form a temporary record. Their preservation in Greek conditions is entirely fortuitous, since the clay cracks and becomes friable (i.e. apt to crumble) with the passage of time and changing humidity. Those tablets which are preserved were accidentally baked in one of the major fires which destroyed the palaces at Pylos and Mycenae, together with the *archive* rooms where the tablets were stored at the time. For this reason the survival of the tablets is entirely random and it is not even possible to tell how complete or representative any particular set of records is. They must, however, be among the most recent finds in any destruction level – records of the transactions during the current year or the past few weeks.

The majority of the preserved tablets belong to the second half of the 13th century BC, just before the disappearance of the Mycenaean palace centres. So far only very few date from earlier Mycenaean contexts on the mainland, and none yet discovered post-date the destructions of c.1200 BC. The tablets from Knossos are conventionally dated to the beginning of the 14th century BC, a date which, together with that of the destruction of the palace at Knossos, is disputed by several scholars.

There are two basic types of record which account for most of the tablets. The first is the instant record of transactions – entries with a name, commodity and quantity – perhaps only one to a tablet. These tablets are long thin bars known as *leaf* tablets (Fig. 15). Their contents might then be copied on to a larger document, a rectangular *page* tablet which would be given a heading and sometimes a total, in addition to the individual entries, to form a longer term record. This could not be done from the start since the clay would all too readily dry out between entries in the heat of a Greek summer. Fortunately, in a small number of cases, both sets of records are preserved to help us understand the system. It is likely, but cannot be proved, that these records in turn were consolidated into complete documents written on some other material such as parchment or papyrus, for the linear script of the tablets is not well suited to clay and may have been devised for something nearer pen and ink. If the intention of the palace authorities was to set quotas and check these from year to year against actual tithes paid or supplies issued, the clay tablets would be too unwieldy and fragile an archive.

Despite the random preservation, the tablets provide us with a vivid insight into the mechanics of the Mycenaean system of administration and the extent to which the bureaucracy of the palaces reached into every sphere of life and activity. There are few kinds of item which do not appear to have been listed or counted, issued or received by the administrators. The system of record-keeping also extended beyond the confines of the palace. However, just as palatial control did not reach to every part of Mycenaean Greece in the 13th century BC, it is likely that the administration was concerned only with those who worked directly for it. A hierarchy of officials, some with almost recognisable Greek titles, is indicated by many sets of tablets. These officials may have been estate holders, responsible for large areas of the 'kingdom'.

The contribution of the written texts to understanding aspects of Mycenaean crafts and technology has already been mentioned. They provide information about the underlying economy of stockraising and farming which supported all the other activities of craftsmen and workers who are mentioned, from bronzesmiths to bakers. They enable some understanding of social and military organisation, or of the production of perishable commodities such as cloth and perfume, which appear to have been important 'exports' basic to long-range trade. In another sphere, they provide a temple inventory and the names of many divinities familiar in the Olympian Pantheon.

Agriculture and stockraising

In studying any prehistoric society, it is only too easy to focus on the upper levels of society and neglect the majority of the population. Durable monuments and striking examples of material culture were often created for the rich and powerful. While we may marvel at the wealth of gold deposited in the early Mycenaean Shaft Graves, we must not forget the vast numbers of farmers and craftsmen whose labour and produce made it possible. Although surviving archaeological evidence is scant, it is sufficient, in combination with large numbers of Linear B tablets recording animals and agricultural produce, to produce a surprisingly clear picture of ordinary activities in the Mycenaean Palatial period. In reconstructing this picture of the most vital part of the economy, usually known to archaeologists as the *subsistence economy*, it is essential to take into account the nature of the Greek landscape and climate.

Landscape and climate

The landscape of southern Greece is varied and often rugged. High limestone mountain ranges running NNW-SSE divide it into small, distinct regions. Winter snowfall on the mountains feeds rivers which vary from impassable torrents in spring to dry beds in autumn. In lowland areas, the winters are mild, with moderate rainfall in the west, decreasing in the more arid eastern districts. In summer, every region is hot and rainfall minimal between May and November. Good, well watered, agricultural land is restricted to plains such as that of Argos between Mycenae and the sea, the river valley of the Eurotas with Sparta at its heart, or the coastal plain of Messenia in the south-west of the Peloponnese. These, unsurprisingly, were the areas where Mycenaean civilization first flourished. Above the plains, the soil cover is thin and often of poor quality. Before the impact of farming some nine thousand years ago, the whole landscape could support large areas of natural forest and woodland. Today only a few small areas survive on the higher slopes.

Crops

Cereals were the principal crop. Barley grew in every area and wheat, with its greater yield, wherever enough rainfall or soil moisture could bring it to a successful harvest in the early summer. In some places extensive provision was made for storage in huge clay jars (pithoi), though nowhere is this as striking as at Knossos. Grains of several varieties of these crops often survive through accidental charring, (because charcoal does not decay). The Linear B tablets record large quantities of both wheat and barley, received into the palace storerooms or issued as rations to different groups of workers. Some tablets indicate both public and private landholdings, and the differing amounts assigned to different officials shows the relative importance of each official.

This combination of evidence suggests strongly that the palaces fostered the surplus production of cereals and, through tithes or some other form of taxation, gathered it into centrally controlled granaries, where it was available not only to support palace craftsmen and 'public' services but also to provide a reserve in times of crop failure. The biblical story of Joseph persuading the Egyptian Pharaoh to store the plenty of seven years against the hard times to come reflects a similar provision. Although it is set in a different landscape and culture, it provides an image of the central organisation of an 'insurance policy' which seems to have underlain both the Mycenaean civilization and the Minoan which preceded it. It is, in fact, more appropriate to a Greek context where crops depend on rainfall than to Egypt where the annual Nile floods formed the basis of agricultural success. It is perhaps even more pertinent when we remember that Joseph was from Palestine, which has a climate not unlike that of Greece.

Granaries containing large quantities of charred wheat and barley, as well as other crops, were discovered at a contemporary Bronze Age settlement in Northern Greece, Assiros. This site, although beyond the limits of the Mycenaean heartland, illustrates the practice of central crop storage on a smaller scale. Here, the quantity stored was far in excess of the needs of the estimated maximum number of inhabitants who could have lived at this small site and it must have represented the surplus of a considerable part of the surrounding area.

Other annual crops, apart from cereals, included legumes such as lentils, beans, peas and vetch, today familiar only as animal fodder. The Linear B records add other items to this list which rarely survive as seeds, especially aromatics such as cumin, coriander and sesame.

An important aspect of Mediterranean farming, less familiar to those of us who live in northern Europe, (at least until the advent of global warming!), is the use of the long-term crops, olives and grapes, which are an essential part of the traditional way of life. Although their introduction transformed the potential for human exploitation of unpromising areas in southern Greece, it is still not certain when domesticated varieties were first used – though they were well established by the Mycenaean period. Olive trees cannot tolerate hard winters and will not grow at high altitudes or in most areas of northern Greece away from the coast. Olives and vines, which need several years to start producing fruit and live for a long time, are both indicators of stability of landholding while their economic importance is threefold. Firstly, they can be grown with limited rainfall and on relatively poor ground. In the case of the olive, cereals can be grown between the trees so that the use of limited agricultural land can be maximised. Secondly, their crops are harvested at different times of the year from cereals – grapes in the autumn, olives in the winter – so that manpower can be productively exploited throughout the year. Thirdly, they both provide storable crops – olives as oil, and grapes as dried raisins or fermented wine – to supplement (and enliven) the diet throughout the year and to provide additional insurance against the failure of other crops. Oil and wine are both well represented on the tablets, and at Pylos, in particular, large areas were shown to be devoted to oil and wine storage. The oil provided in addition to its food value an important ingredient for one of the palace industries: the production of perfumed oil and ointment. Special oil jars with Linear B inscriptions painted on them were transported from one centre to another throughout southern Greece to meet this demand for the raw material.

Other tree crops such as pears and almonds, whose charred seeds survive, and figs are mentioned in the tablets in large quantities. Stored dry, as well as eaten fresh, they provided an important supplement to the diet long after harvesting. Other fruits will also have been collected.

Animals

From the introduction of farming to Greece about 9000 years ago, sheep and goats formed the majority of the domestic animals which were reared, though neither are native to the area. The collections of animal bones from Mycenaean sites show that about three-quarters were from sheep and goats, while domesticated pigs and cattle, the animals native to Greece's natural woodland, were less common. All are mentioned in the tablets in varying numbers and male and female are usually differentiated in the ideograms. The Homeric emphasis on cattle as the most important of animals may reflect their status and value but certainly not their frequency. As today, the flesh of these animals, their hides and even their bones, were all valued for different purposes. Meat was however probably less common on the Mycenaean dinner menu than the Homeric emphasis on massive sacrifices and heroic feasting would suggest – but perhaps not all Mycenaeans were heroes!

The renewable, *secondary products* of these animals were almost more important. Milk and its storable form cheese, from cows, sheep and goats, leave no archaeological traces but they were certainly exploited. Wool and cloth are both regularly recorded on the tablets, and there is a very important series from Knossos which lists nearly a hundred thousand sheep in flocks in several parts of Crete. While these records only represent the current year's census and are, in any case, incomplete, the economic importance of these flocks to the Knossian economy is abundantly clear. Arthur Evans had suggested, before the tablets were deciphered as Greek, that the recognisable ideograms and numbers related to the performance of massive ritual sacrifices at some great festival. The fact that all were recorded as *male* seemed to fit this interpretation: no sensible farmer would have ten rams in his flock, let alone ten thousand. A persuasive and more practical alternative is that these male sheep are in fact *wethers* (castrated males), kept for their wool – as was the case in the great wool-producing districts of mediaeval England.

On this basis, the existence of a second major palace industry – cloth production – has been proposed. This would fit well with the Egyptian wall-paintings depicting Aegean tributaries who have brought bales of cloth as well as objects of silver and gold (Chapter 10). The story of Penelope in the *Odyssey* weaving a magnificent shroud for Laertes, and the gullibility of the suitors in not questioning the time it was taking, remind us that elaborately woven textiles could be luxury products.

There are also references at Pylos to flax and flax-workers, suggesting the production of linen, appropriate in an area where water is more abundant both for growing the crops and for *retting* (rotting the stems to release the fibres), and where the industry has continued to the present day.

Cattle were probably the normal traction animals for wagons or ploughing and at Knossos, at least, some plough oxen were given names such as Dapple, Dusky or Whitefoot. Horse bones are infrequently found – with the exception of those horse burials which represent the favourite chariot teams of the very wealthy. The tablets, however, list numbers of horses, usually in the context of military equipment (Chapter 8). Goats and pigs are mentioned quite frequently on the tablets. Dogs are shown in some of the hunting scenes and their bones are a regular if not common find, but cats had probably not yet been introduced from Egypt or the Near East – even if seen in Cretan wall-painting. Bee-keepers are recorded together with the production of honey.

Animal bones also show us that hunting was practised quite extensively for furs as well as for meat. A wide range of wild animals is represented, from the deer of different varieties to the wild boar whose tusks were used for helmets, or smaller animals such as foxes and hares. The few finds of the fragile bones of game birds such as ducks and geese are enough to show that they were also regularly hunted. (Finds of chicken bones at Tiryns owe more to the excavators' lunches earlier this century than to their early introduction in Greece. The chicken take-away first appears in the Archaic period, some six hundred years later). Fish, represented by occasional finds of their very fragile bones, and edible snails added to the variety of the cuisine. Even lion bones have been found to confirm the pictures of lion hunts in different forms of art.

Fig. 16 Lion hunting on gold 'cushion' seals from Shaft Grave III at Mycenae, c. 1550 BC: a) lion and warrior, l. 1.9 cm. b) lion wounded by arrow, l. 2.1 cm.

Slaves and workers

It is unlikely that the palaces controlled all areas or all aspects of life directly. While it can be assumed that large numbers of families existed whose life was devoted simply to staying alive on their farms, few graves can be attributed to this class of society, and they are not mentioned directly on the tablets. Some information, however, is available about that part of the population whose lives and livelihood depended on the palaces. There are clear references to slave women, engaged in activities such as textile production at Knossos and as spinners, flax-workers or bath attendants at Pylos, often with an adjective referring to their place of origin: 'women of Miletus', for example. Sometimes they are accompanied by a number of children. Some slaves are listed with reference to their owners, whether officials, craftsmen or divinities. In the latter case they seem to have a status which suggests that the term 'slave' and title 'Servant' were interchangeable. Some men, though it is not known whether they were free or slaves, receive larger rations which suggest that they had families to be supported – and to help in their allotted work.

Officials and administrators

The rich grave-goods in many of the family tombs show the existence of a class of wealthy people. The tablets provide the titles of officials, presumably of this class. The landholdings recorded for such officials as *basileus* (? petty king as in Odysseus' Ithaca) *lawagetas* (leader of the people), *telestai, hequetai* (followers), or *koreter* and *prokoreter* (governor and deputy governor), listed at Pylos, allow them to be ranked in importance and their roles as central and local administrators, or as military commanders and religious functionaries, to be explored.

Finally the title *wanax* (frequently as an epithet for Agamemnon in Homer, as in the phrase *anax andrōn*, 'lord of men') seems to refer in many cases to the 'king' himself as a landholder. Sometimes it is used in a context which suggests that it is an epithet for a divinity and it may be that, as in Egypt or in later imperial Rome, the dividing line between kingship and divinity was a narrow one. Doubtless each ruler manipulated the cult practices and beliefs of the community to support his authority and present the beneficence of the gods as a result of his own intervention. The role of religion in Mycenaean society was probably very important but the evidence which survives presents a confusing and tantalising picture (Chapter 11).

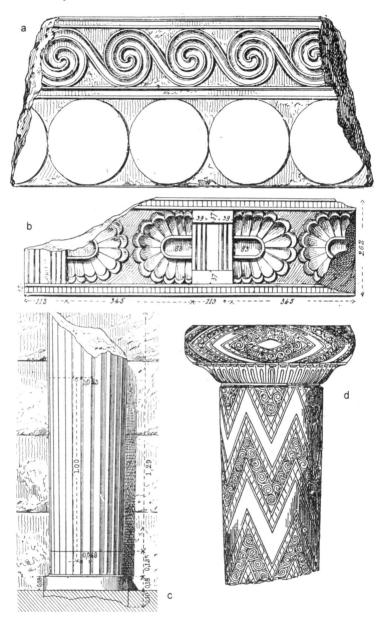

Fig. 17 a) and b) fragments of facade of Treasury of Atreus in green and and red stone; c) half-column in gypsum from Clytemnestra tholos, ht 1.6m; d) half-column from Treasury of Atreus in grey-green stone.

Chapter 7
Building and engineering

Tholoi

In the Early Mycenaean period, the greatest efforts of craftsmen and engineers were reserved for the monumental tholos tombs. At Mycenae there were nine tholoi, each built with increasing elaboration. Considerable expertise was needed to erect the vaulted roofs over the circular chambers which, at first, were constructed of rough masonry. As greater skill was developed and experience gained, the tholoi became larger and more ambitious. Dressed masonry was regularly used to build vaults (up to 15m. in diameter and 13.5m. high) and long *dromoi* – entrance passages. Tombs of this type served local rulers throughout southern Greece and further north, as at Dimini in Thessaly.

The vaulting was achieved by corbelling – a technique in which each course of blocks slightly overlaps the one below in order to reduce the span still to be roofed. As the centre of gravity of the whole tended to move beyond its base as each course was added, counterbalances were provided by piling increasing thicknesses of stone and earth around the exterior. Eventually a mound was formed above the tomb. Studies of the interior curvature of tholoi, where a sufficient height was preserved, show that there is, in every case, a standard relationship between the original radius and eventual height. In algebraic terms, for each tomb the *cube* of the radius is directly related to the *square* of the height. The engineers, however, must have developed simple 'rules of thumb' for achieving this consistent curve, which ensures the stability of the whole structure. In some cases, such as the Treasury of Atreus at Mycenae, tholoi have resisted numerous violent earthquakes over the centuries. The use of a constant ratio is a clear indication of a single building tradition, perhaps even of a single group of architect engineers who were summoned as required, in the same way that only a small number of architects were responsible for the great temples of Classical Greece.

The largest of the tholoi, such as the Treasury of Atreus or that at Orchomenos, which were probably built between 1350 and 1300 BC, required enormous amounts of labour for quarrying and hammer-dressing stone blocks often 3m. in length, and for dragging these into position with the aid of ramps and rollers. The 8m. long outer lintel block alone is calculated to weigh over 100 tonnes.

Once built, these large tholoi were lavishly decorated. The facade of the Treasury of Atreus was embellished with half-columns and decorated with carved spirals, rosettes and zigzags (Fig. 17 p. 54). The stone for these decorative elements, including the 8.5m. long column shafts, was brought from quarries many kilometres away. Probably brought most of the way by sea, they would have been hauled 15km. from the coast across the Argive plain to Mycenae. Similar craftsmanship is seen in the ceiling (Fig. 18) of the side chamber of the ruined tholos at Orchomenos to the north of Thebes in central Greece. Both these tombs were reported to have bronze plates or decorative plaques nailed to their interiors.

Fig. 18 Fragment of ceiling block from side chamber of Orchomenos tholos in greenish limestone. The whole ceiling measured c. 3.7 x 2.7m. The design is thought to reflect textiles or carpets used as wall and ceiling hangings, an idea perhaps shared with Egypt, where Mycenaean textiles are sometimes painted on tomb ceilings.

All these tholoi must have needed months if not years for their construction. Presumably most were built during the lifetime of their 'owner' and left open to demonstrate his power and importance. All the more elaborate examples have hinge-sockets and bolt holes for doors at the entrance. Whilst it is likely that the dromoi of humbler chamber tombs

(Chapter 4) were filled in once the burial was made and the door blocked with a stone wall, the imposing entrances of the tholoi were surely not intended to be hidden. The side chambers at Mycenae and Orchomenos may have been used for the burial itself while the main chamber could have served as a mortuary chapel in the manner of Egyptian royal burials. Indeed, the idea of monumental tombs as symbols of power could well have been derived from the knowledge of the pyramids of Egypt.

Fortresses

The great fortresses built by the Mycenaeans are among the most enduring monuments to their resources, skills and ingenuity. They were a source of wonder to the Greeks of the Classical period and to travellers throughout the ages. With the progress of archaeological research many other examples of their achievements in building and engineering have been recognised.

The ancient Greeks called the fortress walls 'Cyclopean' because of the legends of the Cyclopes who, it is told, assisted Perseus with the construction of the walls of Mycenae. The massive unshaped blocks of limestone, piled on top of each other with close-fitting joints, seemed too much for mere mortal men to achieve. We now know that the Mycenaeans were not superhuman but simply ingenious and persistent. The fortresses at Mycenae, Tiryns, Athens and many other sites were built on craggy hilltops from which the limestone blocks could be prised with levers and moved only a short distance to their place on the 5m. thick walls. Many blocks were rolled down from above, while some were raised into place from below with the aid of earth ramps. Bronze tools were inadequate for cutting the hard limestone and dressed masonry was only used for effect, as for example around the Lion Gate at Mycenae, where a different kind of stone – conglomerate – was hammered or sawn and polished into shape at the cost of much time and labour (Fig. 19, overleaf). Some of the circuits are of vast extent – at Midea south of Mycenae, and Gla north of Thebes, for example, there are walls nearly three kilometres long. The walls avoid the difficulties created by a change of slope or the passage of a water course by following the contours of the chosen hill. Sometimes the joints can be seen where one gang of labourers finished their stretch and another started. The construction of walls like this required vast numbers of labourers and their demolition was almost as difficult. Though the gateways may have been damaged and a few breaches made in the fortress walls in the destructions around 1200 BC, these gaps were readily filled and several of the walls

a

b

Note that the Bristol Classical Press logo (title page) shows another sealstone, from Chamber Tomb 8 at Mycenae, of sardonyx with 'lions' posed like those on the Lion Gate, but sharing a single head, diam 2.1cm.

Fig. 19 a) Lion Gate at Mycenae, 13th century BC; b) agate seal from Chamber Tomb 58 at Mycenae, with griffins in similar heraldic pose, together with altar and column, diam 2.0cm.

provided shelter for generations to come. This can best be seen at Athens, where the Mycenaean walls survived as the defences of the Acropolis until extensively demolished by the Persians during their sack of the city and its temples in 480 BC. Fragments of the Cyclopean masonry can still be seen in places, encased in the Classical walls.

Within the citadel at Tiryns, chambers were left in the thickness of the walls to provide accommodation or storage and, at the south end, two sets of galleries were formed by linking a row of such chambers with covered passages (Fig. 20). The roofs of these galleries were simply formed by leaning massive blocks together so that those on either side supported each other. Cyclopean masonry on a smaller scale was also used for the supporting terraces below major houses inside and outside the walls at Mycenae, and for the creation of tunnels leading to the protected water supplies at Mycenae and Tiryns.

Fig. 20 Tiryns, the SE galleries, c. 1230 BC. Built in Cyclopean masonry, the roof of the passage and of the chambers opening off it were formed with a simple version of the corbelling technique.

Roads and waterworks

The same building techniques were used for other structures. Traces of Mycenaean roads, wide enough to take wagons, can still be found around

Mycenae itself. Like the fortifications, these usually follow the contours and use gentle gradients. Streams were crossed with bridges whose massive blocks still resist the flow of water while the gaps between them allow its passage. Other engineering works have been noted to the east of Tiryns where tens of thousands of tons of earth were moved to form a dam and divert a torrent into a new bed, which took the flow well away from the citadel and the town surrounding it. The stream still follows the new bed today. In Lake Copais, before the drainage works of the 1920's, the remains of earlier ditches and embankments could be seen which belonged to a Mycenaean drainage scheme carried out in the 13th century BC, at the same time that the great fortress of Gla was built on a rocky island in the former lake. The excess water was carried away towards the sea through a rock-cut tunnel several kilometres in length.

Palaces

The Mycenaean palace buildings must have been imposing. Courtyards and colonnades led to the great hall at their centre, known as a megaron after the Homeric term for the king's hall. Smaller than their Minoan predecessors, the focus is different – the megaron with its central hearth rather than an open courtyard. The best preserved example is the 13th-century BC Palace of Nestor at Pylos (Fig. 5, p. 20). Here a complex of buildings of different dates surrounds the palace block with its formal entrance, interior courtyard and megaron flanked by long corridors. On either side there were storerooms and pantries. Like Odysseus' palace as described by Homer (*Odyssey*, especially XXII), it had an upper storey, perhaps for the living quarters of the king and his immediate entourage.

Nothing is known of any palace buildings for the earliest Mycenaean period, though it is likely that wealthy rulers such as those found buried in the Shaft Graves had grand residences. A series of 14th-century BC buildings with side corridors found at the Menelaion site near Sparta may be early versions of the architectural form seen at Pylos. Fragments of wall-paintings from both Mycenae and Tiryns suggest the presence of important buildings there at the same period. In the 13th century BC there were palaces at Mycenae and Tiryns, and there are substantial buildings at Gla as well. Finds of jewellery and Linear B tablets at Thebes, and monumental masonry and tablets at Chania in Crete, mark the sites of their palaces. On the Acropolis at Athens, cuttings in the rock underneath the Erechtheum may be traces of a Mycenaean palace.

Construction techniques

Although these palaces seem to have been lavishly decorated with painted floors and vivid wall-paintings, the construction methods used are essentially practical and can best be seen at Pylos. The lower course of the walls was formed of blocks of soft limestone which could be shaped with bronze saws. The upper surface of this foundation was set with small mortice holes to secure the substantial framework of horizontal and vertical timbers, which, with an infill of mud-brick and clay, formed the remainder of the two-storey structure. Elsewhere, rough masonry was used for the filling of the walls, but the timber framing was ubiquitous and the techniques the same whether for palatial or private buildings.

Four stuccoed wooden columns around the megaron's internal central hearth helped support the upper storey. Similar columns were used in the entrance porches and the colonnade around the courtyard. Some of these columns were fluted as in later Classical temples. Door casings were of dressed timber and the surviving pivot-holes in threshold stones show that the doors were often double in the same manner as Cretan ones. Some rooms had massive threshold blocks cut from hard conglomerate stone, while elsewhere traces of wooden thresholds are preserved. Bronze covers for door pivots have been found at Tiryns and Gla. The list of building materials, on tablet Vn 46 from Pylos, includes a column, a pillar, doorposts, dowels, roof beams and other timbers, some of which are connected with the word 'chimney'. It is suggested that this is a list of some of the materials necessary to construct a megaron with a porch. Clay chimney-pots have been found at several sites.

Walls rarely survive high enough to preserve windows or balconies and little trace of roofing material survives. Although fragments of clay roof tiles from pitched roofs have been discovered at Gla and other sites, the existing illustrations show flat roofs. Clay water spouts to drain roofs and balconies are often found. Floors could be of trodden earth or stuccoed. In important rooms such as the megaron, the stuccoed floors were painted and surrounded with a stone edging, perhaps as a firm base for benches or stools.

Houses

Some Mycenaean towns were very large, but detailed knowledge of them is still limited. At Mycenae, for example, the town had an area of

c. 32 hectares on the slopes to the north, west and southwest of the citadel, but most awaits excavation. The timber and mud-brick used for much of the construction is easily obliterated and Classical and modern towns have often been built on top of Mycenaean sites. Under Thebes there are traces of a Cyclopean wall enclosing an area of c. 30 hectares, including two successive palaces. The remains of several Mycenaean houses have been exposed piecemeal during the rescue excavations which now precede rebuilding and, consequently, it is difficult to understand the town plan. Near Dimini in Thessaly another town with a regular grid of streets has been partially explored, while at Nichoria in Messenia the scant remains of buildings are scattered along a ridge above the plain. It is certain that most communities clustered around a defensible hill like the Menelaion at Sparta, even if Cyclopean walls were not always constructed.

Individual buildings have been explored at Mycenae, both inside and outside the citadel walls. Most of these are well-built – at least in their lower storey – but it is not clear which are palace dependencies and which are 'private' homes. Some have 'palatial' characteristics such as columned porticoes (in the House of the Columns at the south-east end of the citadel at Mycenae), elaborate doorways or wall-paintings. Most were two storeys in height while some, for instance the South House at Mycenae, may even have been three.

The best known examples of houses are on two adjacent terraces on the hill slope to the south of Grave Circle B, perhaps close to the main approach road to the citadel. Although only the foundations and parts of the lower storeys survive, the objects abandoned after a fierce destruction provide clues to the wealth of the owners. In the House of the Oil Merchant the basement level contained seven storerooms opening off a long corridor, with a space for stairs at one end by which they were once reached from the floor above. The storerooms contained large numbers of oil-storage and transport jars, as well as nearly forty Linear B tablets. Immediately to the south is the House of Sphinxes, which contained thousands of pieces of ivory including a plaque decorated with the sphinxes which gave the building its name. This too had storerooms opening off a corridor. To the north, the basement of the House of Shields (named after ivory figure-of-eight shield plaques found there) had a simpler plan. The West House stood on the higher terrace to the west. Without a basement, its ground floor level was equivalent to that of the upper storey of the adjacent House of the Oil Merchant. Its plan included a small paved court with a megaron opening off it. Linear B tablets were also found in this building.

Chapter 8
Weapons and warfare

Homer's principal concerns in the *Iliad* are the deeds of warriors and heroes. From the first discoveries in the Shaft Graves, it was clear that warriors and their equipment were well represented in the Mycenaean world. Swords and spears were characteristic offerings in male interments everywhere, perhaps to equip them for the battles of the next world. In addition to these surviving weapons, wall-paintings, gold rings and ivory plaques illustrate warriors and their equipment, while references in the Linear B texts show the extent to which the palace centres were concerned with equipping their forces. In some cases, the development of particular types of sword or spear can be traced through the Mycenaean period and changes in military practice can be inferred. There are only isolated examples of other types of military equipment. A few battle scenes show the warriors in actual combat. These however, the silver Battle Krater and Siege Rhyton from Mycenae or the battle over a river depicted in a wall painting at Pylos, give no impression of organisation or tactics.

The effectiveness of this armour and these weapons, the skill of their makers and the resources necessary to provide them are beyond doubt. In the discussion that follows, we have described the equipment in the order that a warrior armed himself – as related by Homer in passages where Paris, Agamemnon, Patroclus and Achilles prepare for combat (*Iliad* III, 328-338; XI, 15-46; XVI, 130-144; XIX, 367-391).

Greaves

The earliest examples, made from thin bronze sheet originally worn over a padding of leather or felt, formed part of the 14th-century BC Dendra suit of armour. These covered the leg from ankle to knee and appear to have been held in place by the natural spring of the metal. There are no holes for thonging. A later, shorter pair, more like shin guards, with embossed decoration is from Kallithea in Achaea. This decoration resembles that on breastplates which became familiar in Central Europe at the end of the second millennium BC. Full-length greaves depicted white in wall-paintings, such as the warrior scene from Pylos or the falling man from Mycenae, were perhaps made of thick felt. No example of the type described by Homer (*Iliad* XIX, 367-391) as of 'fine tin' survives either in the Mycenaean period or later.

Cuirass

The earliest surviving complete suit of metal armour from Europe was found in a small chamber tomb at Dendra, south of Mycenae (Fig. 21). Made from sheets of hammered bronze, the breast and back plates were 'tailored' to fit its wearer and hinged together on one side. Additional, three-part, shoulder-pieces were also fitted to the body. The neck was protected by a separate high collar and the lower body by a 'skirt' formed from three overlapping plates front and back. The whole was lined with leather and the edges were bound. The separate parts were held together with rawhide thongs. Although, at first sight, it looks like the 'tin man' in the 'Wizard of Oz', when divested of the additional protection it resembles the later hoplite cuirass. At Dendra it was accompanied by a pair of greaves, a boar's tusk helmet with metal cheek-pieces and a single wrist-guard (perhaps one of a pair since the tomb had been partially looted just prior to excavation). A hand guard with 'buttons' to secure it to the sleeve was found in Chamber Tomb 15 at Mycenae.

Some indication of the frequency of this kind of armour is given by tablets at Knossos and Pylos. At Pylos a minimum of 20 suits is recorded (called *to-ra-ke*, 'thorakes') together with an ideogram of a cuirass and helmet. At Knossos, in the 'chariot tablet' series, a similar ideogram, suggesting breastplate and skirts as found at Dendra, is used to identify at least 140 suits. In some cases, this has been erased and replaced with the ideogram for a bronze ingot as though the ingot and suit of armour were seen as equivalent. (For this reason we reject the suggestion, originally made before the discovery of the Dendra armour, that the tablets recorded cuirasses of heavy layered linen or canvas.) While these tablets may reflect an inventory of the palace armouries, the only existing examples of armour come from 'private' contexts – the complete suit from Dendra, a shoulder-piece from another tomb there and a large part of a complete cuirass from a house at Thebes. The general lack of finds of bronze armour may reflect the ease with which this metal was recycled, whether melted down or, as with the skirt plates, simply reshaped. A forerunner of this armour may be indicated by the two gold breastplates forming part of the regalia found with burials in Grave Circle A.

How practical was this armour? Did it inhibit the wearer in battle and

Fig. 21 Armour: a) sardonyx seal from Shaft Grave III showing figure-of-eight shield, ht 2.5cm;
b) ivory head of warrior with boar's tusk helmet, Mycenae, ht 8cm;
c) bronze armour and boar's tusk helmet from Dendra (see page 64);
d) warriors with tower shields, spears and tasselled scabbards from the miniature frieze on the N wall of Room 5 in the West House at Akrotiri.

what weapons could he use? Despite the cumbersome appearance of the Dendra armour, the separate plates provided both complete protection and considerable flexibility. This has been amply demonstrated by the reconstruction of a full-size suit of armour. It was made using a copper alloy of a similar density to that of the original. We calculate that this could have weighed, like an ingot, about 25kg. Worn with a helmet, the high collar provided full protection for the warrior's face with only a narrow slit left for vision. Even this gap could be closed with a slight shrug.

Experiments show that the heavy shoulder-pieces would effectively have prevented both spear-throwing and archery but that a sword or thrusting spear could have been wielded freely. To assist this the right armhole was cut deeper than the left on the Dendra suit of armour. A fit man in armour, knocked to the ground, can regain his feet with surprising speed. In the heat of battle, however, it would not have been fast enough, as a warrior could only have done this by first turning on his front.

No example of these cuirasses is known from the post-palatial period. Even if the communities of the 12th century could have afforded the outlay of bronze in their reduced economic circumstances, the increasing prevalence of thrown spears or javelins would have rendered armour of this kind less practical.

A different type of metal armour also seemed to have been in use throughout the Mycenaean period. Made from small overlapping scales, it is represented by the discovery of plates at Troy in the 14th century BC and Mycenae in the 12th century BC. This kind of armour is better known in the Near East and Egypt. Clay tablets at the 15th-century BC Hurrian palace of Nusi list scale armour for men and horses, and a cuirass of this type is illustrated in the 15th-century BC tomb of Ken-Amun in Egypt.

Swords and daggers

The swords used by the Mycenaeans include a wide range of types, some of which are rare and thus possibly experimental. The first daggers or knives of the Early Bronze Age were triangular in shape and as time passed they became longer and acquired thick midribs. By the beginning of the Mycenaean period long rapiers with a midrib were common. At first, like the earlier daggers, the hilt end of the blade was rounded and the wooden hilt attached over the blade with rivets (Type A, Fig. 22). Pommels of wood, sometimes covered with gold, or of ivory or stone, plain or decorated, have been found with many of these swords and daggers. Occasionally traces of the scabbards have also been found.

Some swords and daggers had elaborately decorated hilts or blades.

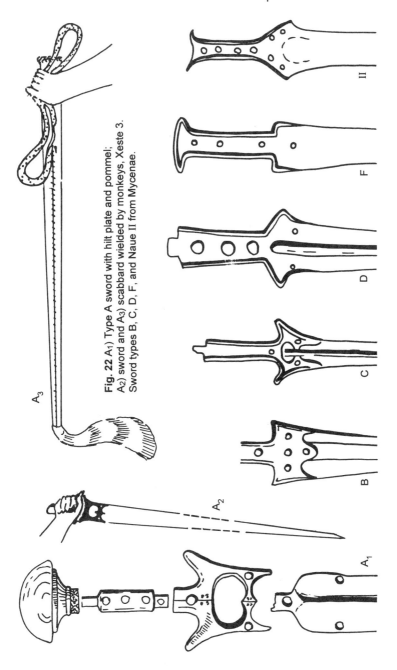

Fig. 22 A₁) Type A sword with hilt plate and pommel; A₂) sword and A₃) scabbard wielded by monkeys, Xeste 3. Sword types B, C, D, F, and Naue II from Mycenae.

Short daggers, ornamented with inlaid scenes in gold, silver and niello are counted among the masterpieces of Aegean craftsmanship (Fig. 12, p. 38).

Weapons of this type had an inherent weakness where the hilt joined the blade, and it is not surprising that this end of the blade was soon extended to provide strength and support for the hilt plates of swords of Type B. The midrib was also thickened to provide greater strength, necessary for blades which could reach 70cm. or more in length. Both kinds of sword are frequent finds in the Shaft Graves. Schliemann reported that Grave V (his sepulchre 1) included 'a large heap of more or less broken bronze swords which may have represented more than sixty entire ones', as well as some twenty-eight others with only three burials.

The next stage in the development was the elaboration of the shoulders of the blade to provide protection for the hand. At first this was achieved by a pair of horns slanting out from the hilt to deflect a glancing blow (Type C), but soon these became standardised as short cruciform projections (Type D). Both forms tended to be shorter than their predecessors and were widely used in Mycenaean Greece and Crete and even in the regions to the north, Epirus, Macedonia and Bulgaria. Occasional examples of daggers with cruciform hilts are also known. By the palatial period, swords had become much shorter, with flat blades, simple square shoulders and a fully-flanged hilt with T-shaped extension to support the pommel as well as the hilt plates. This type (F) was made in a variety of sizes from dagger to short sword.

The final development was prompted by an innovation from Central Europe, a longer, stouter sword with flanged hilt (Naue II, Fig. 22), whose hilt plates were riveted in a horseshoe pattern to the sloping shoulders as well as to the hilt. The first appearance of the Naue II sword can be seen just before the destructions of the late 13th century BC and its arrival may be attributed to the increasing importance of trade along the Adriatic. Even if the first examples were imported, the type was soon made with slight variants in Mycenaean workshops, but it did not wholly replace the native Mycenaean form (Type F) until the beginning of the Iron Age. At this time the Naue II form was adopted in iron and continued as the sole type made throughout the Dark Age.

Shield

With the exception of 12th-century BC bosses and fragments of edging from Kaloriziki in Cyprus and 11th-century BC bosses from Athens and Mouliana, evidence for shields is derived from depictions or models. The lion-hunt dagger from Shaft Grave IV (Fig. 12, p. 38) shows two different types clearly – the '*tower*' and the 'figure-of-eight' forms. (The former got its name from the great shield carried by Ajax which Homer always likens to a tower, *Iliad* VII, 219-223.) The tower form is the only one shown in the contemporary miniature wall-paintings at Thera and it seems that it went out of fashion after the early Mycenaean period. Figure-of-eight shields were in use until the end of the palatial period as the painted examples on the walls at Knossos, Mycenae, Thebes and Tiryns demonstrate. Ivory shield models were frequently used as decorative inlays, as from the 13th-century BC House of Sphinxes at Mycenae, or from Delos. Both these types are shown with dappling on them to represent raw oxhide, probably mounted on a wicker frame. The small shields, round or with a lunate cut-out in the lower edge, as seen on both sides of the 12th-century BC Warrior Vase and on a painted grave stele from Mycenae, are a later development.

Helmet

The helmet most commonly found is that covered with boar's tusk plates – the most striking of all the echoes of Bronze Age practice in Homeric Epic (eg. *Iliad* XI, 261-5). Boar's tusk plates from Shaft Grave I and a gold seal from Grave III, show that these were already in use in the 16th century BC. Numerous finds of plates from Dendra, Mycenae, Knossos and many other sites show the helmet's popularity at the height of the Mycenaean period. Ivory plaques showing helmeted warrior's heads (Fig. 21) have been found in Crete as well as at Mycenae and Spata in Attica. Helmets are regularly shown in the wall-paintings, especially the battle scene at Pylos and on a female warrior accompanied by a griffin at Mycenae. Many representations show crests or plumes on the helmets, of which the most elaborate are shown on the Battle krater from Mycenae. Even after the fall of the palaces some were still worn, to judge from recent finds at Knossos and Elateia in Central Greece, which belong to the very end of the Mycenaean period.

Boar's tusk plates are hard and resilient (not unlike the ceramic plates in modern bullet-proof jackets), but they were hard to come by. An adult wild boar has two long curving tusks, each yielding on average six plates when split into segments. Full helmets with three rows of plates need around sixty segments – requiring the hunting of ten or more animals. Since the wild boar was, and still is, one of the most dangerous animals to hunt, obtaining enough tusks to make a helmet needed skill and courage. It is not hard to imagine a young would-be-warrior literally hunting down his own helmet to demonstrate his right to join his elders in the front line of battle. Perhaps this is the significance of the boar-hunt scene from Tiryns!

At Dendra, and Ialysos on Rhodes, the tusks were supplemented by bronze cheek-pieces; but the only fully bronze helmets known include one from 14th-century BC Knossos, where a knobbed helmet has very similar cheek-pieces. An ideogram which resembles this is to be seen on a Linear B tablet from the same site. A second bronze helmet dating to the 11th century BC was found at Tiryns where it is little more than a decorative plate to cover a leather cap. Full bronze helmets may be represented on a damaged ivory plaque found near Grave Rho in Grave Circle B and on the Minoan 'Boxer Rhyton' from Agia Triada. The Warrior Vase shows a different type of helmet, perhaps of leather with a crest and horns.

Homer uses four different names and several epithets for the helmets worn at Troy, which are always envisaged as metal – shining in the sun or ringing when struck. The boar's tusk helmet was, for him, a curiosity.

Spear/Lance

For the Mycenaean warrior, as much as the Homeric hero, the heavy spear was an essential item of equipment. These were weapons for thrusting rather than throwing and the spearhead could be as much as 60cm. in length. They had heavy oval blades with hammered sockets, split to hold a wooden shaft, and are regular finds in the Shaft Graves. A few examples were much smaller – perhaps lances or javelins, but the standard type remained unchanged until the end of the palatial period. A Linear B tablet from Knossos refers to a total of 42 spears with bronze points, while tablets at Pylos require local officials to contribute specific weights of bronze suitable for spears as well as for arrows and ships (? ship fittings). Wall-paintings and other illustrations show spears in use in battle. Sometimes the warriors carry two spears, as described by Homer. In the 12th century BC, the smaller 'javelin' heads with cast sockets become common finds, especially in NW Greece. This type became popular in Central Europe at approximately the same time and provides another instance of contact via the Adriatic sea.

Bow

Although the bow must have been a weapon of great antiquity it is rarely preserved archaeologically. In the Mycenaean period, its use is obvious from representations on a gold ring from Shaft Grave IV, of archers hunting from a chariot or in front of the city walls on the Siege Rhyton, for example, and from the bronze, chert or obsidian arrowheads frequently found in graves from all over the Mycenaean area. Five bowmakers are recorded on a tablet listing tradesmen at Pylos, while tablets at Knossos mention goats' horns, leather and wax, perhaps for making composite bows. For Homer, the bow is rarely a weapon of the battlefield, and only used by a few heroes, though it was, of course, central to the story of Odysseus' revenge on the suitors (*Odyssey* XXI).

Chariot

The idea of the chariot is likely to have been introduced from Syria around the beginning of the Mycenaean period. It can first be seen on one of the grave stelai from Mycenae and on a gold ring from Shaft Grave IV. By the 14th and 13th centuries BC, it had become a popular motif in wall-paintings, on pottery and in miniature figurines. Although usually represented schematically, its main features are clear: four-spoked wheels, a light hide-covered body over a wicker frame with a woven rawhide floor and a single pole. So far no chariot fragments have survived but horse burials in pairs are known from several sites, presumably favourite chariot teams, while bronze horse bits have been found at Mycenae and Thebes. On the evidence of the Linear B tablets, the palaces had astonishing numbers available. At Knossos they list parts such as wheels or frames for hundreds of chariots, presumably kept in the central stores to equip the palace forces, as well as individual inventories recording a name, a chariot and horses, and suits of armour. At Pylos, the records list 117 pairs of wheels of different types, both serviceable and unserviceable. (The parking problem at both palaces must have been solved by storing them dismantled.)

Presumably Homer envisaged a similar light-weight vehicle, readily dismantled for carrying over rough ground or mountain passes, provided by Nestor at Pylos to take Telemachus to Sparta for news of his father (*Odyssey* III, 477-497). It is hard to know how much the story of their two-day journey owes to poetic licence – a proper speed for a hero to travel – and how much to memory of the Mycenaean period, when at least some roads suitable for wheeled vehicles will have existed.

Warfare

Homer's vivid images of battle give the impression of a general mêlée of fighting men without the formations or discipline of the later hoplites. Poetic imagery demands the isolation of individual heroes, 'taxied' by chariots onto the battle field in their heavy armour, engaged in single combat, slain, if their fate so decreed, and buried with signal honours. This may well reflect 8th-century BC practice more than that of the Bronze Age, but the images cannot be too far removed from the Mycenaean reality. Although weapons in graves are frequent, they are by no means universal, and it is likely that only a small proportion of any community was well equipped. The majority can only have been, at best, lightly armed, perhaps often as archers. There must have been some discipline and the use of the large tower shields may imply the existence of formations of men who used their shields to form a protective wall. A formation of this kind is suggested by a row of warriors with tower shields and boar's tusk helmets in one of the scenes from the 'Ship Fresco' at Akrotiri on Thera (Fig. 21, p. 65). The heavy Mycenaean spears are more likely to have been used as pikes for stabbing than for effective throwing – acknowledged by Homer to be an heroic activity. The slender blades of the early rapiers must have been used in a similar way. While the line was intact there could have been little room to wield such long weapons. Once it broke, short daggers were both offensive and defensive weapons. As time passed, swords became shorter and stouter – more suited to cutting and slashing in hand-to-hand fighting than in close formation. The final development, seen in the Naue II sword of the 12th century BC and later, was of a longer, but still stout, sword giving both reach and power to any blow. At the same time the lighter spears or javelins became more popular than the heavy spears of the early period, indicating that battles had become less static and more mobile. Despite the hundreds of chariots recorded at Knossos and Pylos, the terrain of Greece is hardly suited to their use. In battle, they were perhaps more likely to have been prestige transport for royalty and nobility than used as weapons of war.

Hunting was regularly seen in Greece as a noble activity providing both sport and practice in the skills needed for battle. The Mycenaean period is no exception and there are several depictions of hunting scenes with armed warriors on foot or in chariots as on the grave stelai from above the Shaft Graves. Lion and boar were the 'noblest' – and most dangerous – prey, seen on a dagger from Shaft Grave IV or in a wall-painting from the palace at Tiryns. Deer were more common prey, as confirmed by the finds of their bones at most Mycenaean sites, and huntsmen appear to be recorded on the Pylos tablets.

Military planning

The archives of Knossos and of Pylos give some idea of the equipment provided by the palace centres for their military forces and occasionally a glimpse of the men themselves. The lists of weapons or armour and of parts for chariots have already been mentioned. At Pylos there seem to be references to the defensive arrangements for the two provinces. Over 600 'rowers' are listed on a group of damaged tablets which perhaps record preparation for a naval operation. This is enough to man between twelve and twenty ships – rather fewer than the ninety led against Troy by Nestor himself. 'Watchers on the coast' totalling at least 800 men are assigned to ten districts. It is not known whether this refers to a single event, perhaps the emergency which led to the destruction of the Palace of Nestor, or whether this was a routine series of military dispositions whose records were brought up to date at intervals. Whichever is correct, the palace centres, where they existed, played a major part in military organisation. A more individual glimpse of a soldier can be seen in a lively illustration of a kilted man wearing greaves and in the act of drawing his sword, sketched on the reverse of a wet clay tablet (Fig. 16d, p. 46). This was the work of a scribe at Mycenae passing his time watching manoeuvres in the courtyard, while waiting to record the next consignment of wool.

The leaders of Mycenaean society were concerned not only to equip their forces but also to defend their palace centres. To this end, in the 13th century BC, they erected vast fortified circuits at Mycenae, Athens and Gla in central Greece and many other places. The scale of these massive engineering works has already been mentioned (Chapter 7). That their function was solely military, however, is questionable. A purely defensive role, in an era when siege-engines were unknown, would have been served by much slighter walls with much less effort. Part of their function must have been to demonstrate the power and invincibility of the ruler – a characteristic shared with their eastern neighbours at Troy or Hittite Hattusas (Boğazköy). Sieges of such fortress cities are found in art: for example, the silver rhyton and a fragment of wall-painting from Mycenae, and, of course, the Homeric story of Troy itself centres around the 'siege' of such a city. Protracted sieges were probably not normal, although the rulers of three Mycenaean citadels, Mycenae, Tiryns and Athens, did take considerable pains, at the end of the 13th century BC, to secure a water supply accessible from within the walls. Whether their value was ever put to the test is unknown. Soon after the destruction of the palaces at Mycenae and Tiryns around 1200 BC they were out of use and filled with debris. Not for another 600 years were large armies assembled or major fortifications constructed in Greece.

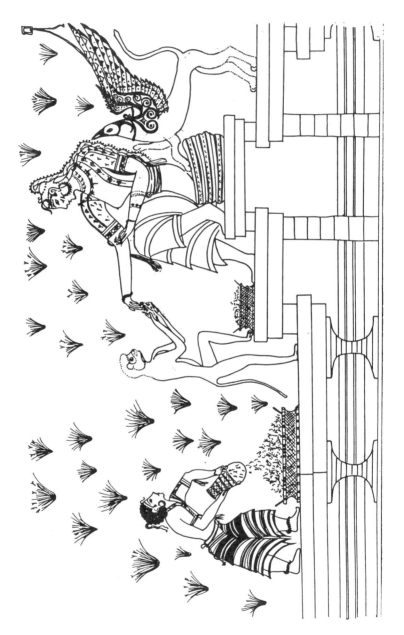

Fig. 23 Saffron gathering scene from Xeste 3, Akrotiri, Room 3a first floor, N wall c. 1500 BC (see page 84).

Chapter 9
Wall-paintings

The interiors of Mycenaean buildings were very colourful. The walls, ceilings, pillars, hearths and even the floors were painted with geometric motifs or representative scenes. These provide some idea of how the Mycenaeans wished to see themselves, which is not necessarily a true representation of everyday life. So far, the most elaborate decoration is found in the palaces and the larger houses. However, as the mud-brick used in almost all buildings needed protecting with plaster, even the smaller houses often had plain painted walls. Occasionally, painted plaster was employed to embellish rock-cut chamber tombs, grave stelai or the famous stone larnax from Agia Triada in Crete (see Chapter 11). The same technique was also used for smaller items such as offering tables.

In official buildings, both upper storey and ground floor rooms served a public function, and many were once richly decorated. In domestic buildings, wall-painting was probably restricted to the principal living quarters which were usually on the upper floors. Ground floor walls remained unpainted since the rooms at this level were generally for storage. In the event of a destruction, the upper storey structure collapsed, so that wall-paintings slipped down into the rooms below and were shattered into small fragments.

Enigmatic pieces of these wall-paintings have been found at many Mycenaean sites. On the Greek mainland, as in Crete, most of the paintings exist as small detached fragments which rarely – unlike pottery – join to make the whole composition intelligible. To preserve the decoration of a whole room intact, a particular kind of catastrophe needs to have occurred, such as the volcanic eruption which overwhelmed Akrotiri on the island of Thera. The astonishing state of preservation of the Akrotiri paintings, first discovered in 1971, has helped the understanding of the place of many small fragments found in earlier excavations from both Crete and the mainland. For this reason we have included here discussion of some of these Theran wall-paintings although they are Cycladic rather than Mycenaean. They are superbly illustrated in Chr. Doumas, *The Wall Paintings of Thera*, (Athens, 1992) – a must for any library covering the history of art. It has proved invaluable for the drawings prepared for this book.

Origins and associations

The earliest known Aegean Bronze Age wall-paintings are probably a few fragments from Crete dating to the 17th century BC. Those from Akrotiri on Thera belong to the late 17th or early 16th centuries while the majority of those from Crete, as well as those from Melos and Keos, belong to the late 16th and 15th centuries. A few pieces from Mycenae, Thebes and perhaps Tiryns may be contemporary with the final use of the Knossos palace in the early 14th century, but the majority from the mainland date to the late 14th and 13th centuries BC.

The exact relationship between Cretan and mainland wall-paintings, or between those of Akrotiri and Crete, is the subject of lively but largely unproductive discussion. Given the small number of pieces, their generally fragmentary nature and the freedom of artistic interpretation used in the reconstructions, it is hard to justify even the frequently made statement that Cretan painting is more naturalistic and Mycenaean more stylised. This view fails to take account of the long interval between Cretan paintings and those from the mainland, the coexistence of naturalistic and stylised paintings at Akrotiri and Pylos and changes in fashion. Something which is less evident at first sight is the extent to which many of the better known and well-illustrated wall-paintings are pastiches created from numerous fragments by the skill of the modern restorers and artists.

The well-known bosomy lady from Tiryns carrying a *pyxis* (cylindrical box) was actually restored on paper by the artist Gillieron from many fragments of different figures. This *composite* image of a woman has thus come to represent all the *individual* figures in a processional fresco of at least eight women. While the restorations are, on the whole, both masterly and correct, inevitably the style of the restorer plays a large, but unacknowledged, part in discussions of the style of Minoan or Mycenaean artists. Words like good versus bad or high, naturalistic or artistic versus decadent, incompetent or debased, spring from personal preference, often heavily influenced by the restoration itself. Only with the survival of large areas of wall-painting as at Thera and Mycenae can the work and style of the original artist be seen uninterpreted.

As in so many areas of Bronze Age art, it seems more appropriate to define wall-painting as Aegean rather than Cretan or Mycenaean. At Knossos the problem is even harder to grasp, since it is not known which paintings were on the walls before the (hypothetical) Mycenaean domination, and which were painted subsequently. For example, the decoration of the Throne Room is often alleged to be Mycenaean. Surely it is of greater interest that such complex and accomplished works of art were executed at this early period, fully-formed and apparently with no earlier period of experiment in the Aegean area, however unlikely this may seem. Only future excavation can hope to clarify the issue.

Wall-painting may owe some debt of inspiration to Egyptian paintings, including both the lively styles used in domestic contexts or on papyri and the more formal painting of processions or funerary scenes in the Egyptian tombs. Direct comparison is, however, difficult since the use in each region was so different. The appreciation of the close relationship between the two areas has been deepened by the recent discovery of fragments of 'Minoan' style wall-paintings at Tell el-Dab'a (Avaris) in the Nile Delta: in particular, a bull-leaping scene and a stylised labyrinth.

Technique

The wall-paintings are usually executed on a fine white lime plaster surface, which itself is on a thicker, coarser backing layer. While most of the painting was done on fresh, wet plaster (*buon fresco*) and is well preserved, some details were added later when the plaster had dried (*fresco secco*) and, in consequence, have vanished or are very faint. Occasionally, the yellow-ochre cartoon can be seen underneath the finished painting, or the impressions of string setting-out lines are preserved in the plaster. No trace of any organic binding medium, such as the egg white used in *tempera*, has been detected by analysis.

A typical Mycenaean palette consists of a full range of colours derived from naturally occurring minerals. Ochres and haematites (sometimes raw, sometimes burnt) were used for all shades from red to yellow, carbon for black, and lime or clay for white (where the background was not sufficient). Infrequently white highlights were obtained by cutting through the colour to the backing plaster. A blue mineral, riebeckite, occurs naturally but the Mycenaeans preferred *Egyptian blue* (a copper oxide compound) which was manufactured specially. Ground lapis lazuli was used on the Agia Triada larnax. Green was either obtained by mixing blue with ochre or by grinding malachite. Other shades needed were obtained by mixing.

Hands and artists

No individual 'hands' have been identified as yet, but it is obvious from Akrotiri, alone, that many different artists contributed to the work. The

Aegean artists were generally competent and some were outstanding. All shared a similar set of conventions, such as red skin colour for men and white for women, yellow for lions, white for sphinxes and blue for monkeys. Eyes were depicted frontally in a profile head, double chins were used for mature women and shaven heads were painted blue. A three-quarter pose was sometimes attempted, as at Pylos and Thera, but not always with great success, and even in these cases the head remained in profile. A sense of depth was regularly indicated by overlapping figures or objects. Occasionally it is possible to see where a painting was reworked, as for example the bull-leaping scene from Tiryns where three tails can be detected.

Composition and subject matter

The well-preserved houses and wall-paintings at 16th-century Akrotiri provide the best information about how the areas available on the walls were divided up into blocks and how the paintings fitted into them. The long narrow area between the windows and ceiling was ideal for a continuous narrative frieze painted in miniature, such as the Ship Fresco in the West House. The spaces between the windows or doors were suitable for panel paintings of individual subjects at a larger scale like the boxers and fishermen. The dado at the bottom of the wall could be either stone or painted. The remaining areas were available for larger compositions including the 'Spring Fresco' with its lilies and swallows where the rockwork acts as a dado, or the saffron-picking scenes in Xeste 3 (Fig. 23, p. 74). Both of these scenes seem to use the walls without regard for doors or windows. Fragments from the different mainland sites represent a similar repertoire of composition and arrangement, even if very few were found in place.

The **subsidiary decoration** employed a number of common motifs. Blue as a background colour was very popular – perhaps because it was costly and indicated to the observer that no expense had been spared in the decoration of a room or building. Formal decoration of spirals, rockwork or imitation stone, is found in border panels or dados, as in Hall 46 at Pylos where at least three successive layers of plaster were painted in this way. The floors of several of the principal rooms were divided up into squares, painted with different motifs: some simulated stone, others 'feather' patterns, and even dolphins, octopus and cuttle-fish are found. Hearths, like those in the megara at Pylos and Mycenae, were decorated with flames licking round their edges. These were frequently replastered and redecorated. Architectural features such as

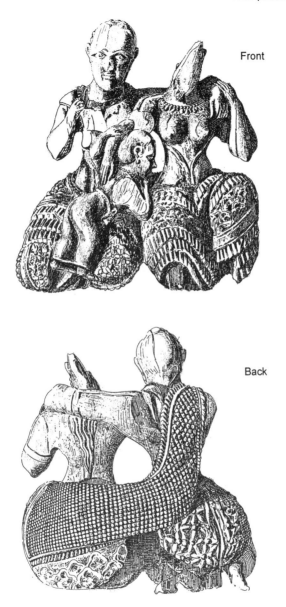

Front

Back

Fig. 24 The Ivory Trio from Mycenae c. 1450 BC. This exquisite piece of carving fully in the round, only 7.6cms high, shows clearly the elaborate textiles of the wrap-over skirts and shawl.

columns were probably painted as was the surround of the central chimney at Pylos in Hall 46, which was decorated with running spirals. A curious quirk of decoration can be seen at Pylos in beams and beam ends which were plastered over and the plaster then painted to represent the wood which had just been covered.

Miniature friezes, between 20 and 50 cms deep, told a story familiar to the Mycenaean observer but today unfortunately unknown. The short-hand narrative style used can be compared to a modern cartoon strip. At Akrotiri, the Ship Fresco shows with great detail a number of ships of different kinds from small cargo ships to large galleys decorated as though for a festival – though the boar's tusk and other types of helmet hanging under the awnings suggest a more sinister purpose. The composition on the south wall reads from left to right with all the boats sailing the same way past one town and towards a second. The population of the second town is waiting, looking towards the flotilla of boats. The small local boats seem to be racing to the shelter of the harbour. Are they bursting with news or running with fear? Is this a much awaited diplomatic mission or a hostile fleet in disguise? The latter theory gains some credence, if read with the fragments from the north wall of the room where armed, boar's-tusk-helmeted warriors march in formation from the shore to a town. In the sea are galleys like those shown on the south wall but this time they bristle with long spears while dead men float in the sea – an accident or a conflict? The further elements of these fragments, the men meeting on the summit of a hill, the animals rounded up or just going out to graze, the women collecting water as an everyday task or in preparation for a siege, serve to underline the difficulty of interpreting this composition, the most narrative of all Aegean wall-paintings. Between these two frescoes on the east wall is a *Nilotic* scene showing a meandering river (perhaps the Nile) with flowers, animals and birds on its banks, which provides a peaceful contrast. Is this part of the story or just decorative? Without the key to the whole, each attempt at interpretation is as valid as the next.

A 13th-century fragment from the Palace at Mycenae shows a detail of a similar town with a (larger) falling warrior while a figure at a window gazes, oblivious, in the opposite direction. Further fragments show more of the town. At Orchomenos, warriors stand on terraces, and at Pylos and Tiryns there are other fragments which suggest the same theme. This theme, perhaps the same story, is also employed in other media such as the silver Siege Rhyton from Shaft Grave IV at Mycenae, decorated in relief, which shows a town with watchers and defenders, ships and drowning men. Whilst it has been suggested that these scenes of towns and warriors are depictions of the best known conflict in the Bronze Age, the Trojan War, the most, sadly, that can definitely be said is that they are of a battle or battles of a kind all too well known in the ancient world.

Other fragments, especially the hunting scenes from Orchomenos, Pylos and Tiryns, and the battle scenes at Pylos could form part of similar narrative compositions but are too fragmentary for this to be more than speculation.

Processional scenes that seem to depict a regular ceremony of people endlessly walking fill the band above the dado. Some were used on stair-cases, as at Knossos and Akrotiri. The participants, sometimes depicted at or near life-size, are either processing to a shrine or deity (which is nowhere preserved), or taking part in a 'diplomatic' ceremony where a ruler is of sufficient status to receive ambassadors and gifts from other potentates, as frequently depicted in Egypt. From the reconstructed fragments, it seems that on the mainland the majority of processional frescoes were of men or women separately. On the sarcophagus from Agia Triada in Crete (Chapter 11), there are both men and women, but even there they are in different zones. Double rows of figures occur, shown either behind or above each other in an attempt to indicate depth. Depth is also shown economically in chariot groups where one horse body serves for two heads and eight legs, while the two figures are shown one behind the other but were in reality side by side. At Thebes, fragments of between nine and twelve women carry objects such as a vase, perhaps made from an ostrich egg, a wooden or ivory pyxis and sprays of flowers. Two similar scenes at different scales existed at Tiryns while at Mycenae there are fragments of more than five including the well known *Mykenaia* (the painting of an elegant lady found near the Cult Centre at Mycenae). At Pylos, there were both male and female processions and a third miniature example said to show both men and a woman accompanying a bull, though the reconstruction of this is not certain. The scene from Pylos with a double register of figures (men and enormous hounds above, men carrying tripod cauldrons below [Fig. 26c, p. 89]), may also be a scene of procession. Fragments, from both Mycenae and Pylos, show *Daemons*, rather than humans, in procession, perhaps as shown on the gold ring from Tiryns (Fig. 32, p. 108).

The fragmentary wall-paintings from the Throne Room at Pylos give some idea of the elements of its decoration. The throne against the north-east wall is thought to have been flanked by a frieze of heraldically posed, overlapping lions and griffins in the same way that the throne at Knossos was flanked by griffins. Further along the wall a spiral-bound pole acts as a panel divider in front of a standing bull. At the south end of the same wall were found fragments showing a lyre-player and an enormous bird.

The player sits on a rock, apparently entertaining four paired male figures half his size seated at tripod tables (Fig. 31, p. 104). It is not clear how this scene, called the 'Bard at the Banquet' by the excavators, relates to the whole. The differing scales may reflect the attempt to show perspective or the lack of connection between the scenes on either side of the pole. A similar frieze of lions and griffins was painted on the walls of another important room (Hall 46) at Pylos with a central hearth like the Throne Room. These were disposed above a painted dado of rockwork and hides, with beams bordering the animal frieze above and below. Above is a band of running spirals just below the ceiling. This decoration extended to all four walls.

Trophy paintings of figure-of-eight shields were used on the walls of both palatial and other buildings at Mycenae, as well as at Thebes and Tiryns. *Ikria* (ships' cabin screens of hide), best known from the West House at Akrotiri, were also used at Mycenae. These designs may have been intended either to impress or to symbolise victory in battle.

Other themes whose associations cannot be established include bull-leaping scenes from Mycenae, Tiryns, Pylos and Avaris, like the better known example from Knossos. Horses and grooms are shown alone at Mycenae and with chariots at Tiryns, while at Pylos there are friezes of dogs and staghunting. Boars are hunted relentlessly at Tiryns, while sphinxes pose riddles at several sites. There are two tantalising fragments from Mycenae, one of which is a hand holding a puppet or figurine (Fig 25). Associated with this piece is a foot on a foot stool. Is the figurine being admired by the woman who is presumably seated, or is it being offered to her by another woman? Could this be the end of a processional fresco as shown on the gold ring from Tiryns?

Cult scenes have been detected in many fragments of wall-painting and, if correctly interpreted, provide valuable information about ritual and religion, as discussed in greater detail in Chapter 11 where several more scenes are described. The only example from the mainland for which a cult scene is a reasonably certain interpretation is the wall-painting from the Room with the Fresco at Mycenae where a large portion was found still attached to the wall. This scene would form the logical end to a processional fresco (Fig. 34, p. 111); unfortunately, the adjacent wall, as far as we know, was unpainted.

The best preserved compositions from the whole Aegean area came from the building called Xeste 3 at Akrotiri on Thera, which to judge by the lack of domestic pottery had some 'official' role. The iconography of the paintings and the presence of a Cretan style *lustral basin* (a sunken basin on the ground floor) hint at a ritual function for these rooms, while the excellent condition of the paintings provides a wealth of information about dress, hairstyle and jewellery (see below).

The most lavishly decorated area, on two storeys, is Room 3, which was divided into two areas on both floors by wooden partitions. The walls of the sunken basin were lined with stone slabs. Above this basin, along the whole length of the north wall, was painted a scene with three women. A long-haired woman, in a tiered wrap-over skirt and a transparent silk top, holds out a necklace towards another seated on a rock, perhaps in a cave. This woman, who is portrayed in a clumsy attempt at a three-quarter pose, has cut her foot and she rests her head in her hand. The third figure, a younger woman, is more concerned with her own adornment as she flings on a sari-like garment while gazing firmly the other way. The central figure is larger, and a loop of her elaborately dressed hair is held by a long pin; a twig of myrtle is tucked into the front of her hair ribbon which is tied in the knotted loop that has come to be known as a *sacral knot*. Unlike all the other female figures in these scenes, she wears no other jewellery apart from hooped earrings. Both hairpin and earrings find parallels in the objects from the Shaft Graves at Mycenae (Fig. 27, p. 92). Her skirt, although tiered, is of a different design to any other overskirt shown in the published frescoes of Thera. All these differences suggest that she was a key figure with a different status.

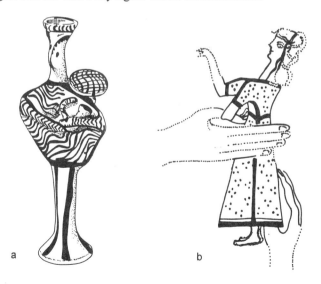

a   b

Fig. 25 a) Clay figurine from Chamber Tomb 41 at Mycenae, ht 13cm, 14th century BC. This elaborate figurine carries two children and a parasol; b) wall-painting from near the Cult Centre at Mycenae showing figurine and hands, ht c. 18cm.

In the western part of the room are three male figures painted in red. The central figure, an adult in a kilt, is pouring from a large jug. To his right, a naked boy with a partially shaved head is carrying a one-handled bowl. On the other side, in a mirror image of the female composition just described, a naked youth looks away and holds an unfolded decorated kilt and a plain white loincloth (Fig. 26, p. 89). Behind him is a small figure painted unusually in yellow ochre, carrying a bowl which is only visible in a faint outline. The whole scene suggests a cleansing ritual.

On the east wall, above the lustral basin, is painted a closed door with lilies whose architrave is decorated with running spirals. The whole gateway is set in a wall of ashlar masonry and surmounted by horns of consecration. The horns and the door are covered with red streaks – to be explained as blood in what must be the only wall-painting with certain ritual significance. If the frescoes are considered to have a unified theme, then, combined with the lustral basin and the depiction of washing and donning of clean clothing, they illustrate scenes of initiation – the passage, perhaps represented by the closed door, from childhood to adulthood or from uninitiated to initiated. It is probable that some of the ceremonies took place in this suite of rooms.

On the upper floor, above the lustral basin, there is a single scene represented on the north and east walls. On the east wall (directly above the gateway) two young women in a rocky landscape are picking *saffron* (crocus stamens). Both are conventionally dressed in tiered wrap-over skirts and bodices. One girl with short curly hair, carrying a basket, is older than the other who has a shaven head. The composition and the rocky landscape continue round the corner where there is a third girl, also with short curly hair (Fig. 23, p. 74). She carries a full basket of saffron on her shoulder as if she is moving towards the central figure of the composition – a richly attired woman seated on three cushions, placed on a tripartite structure. This woman receives, as if testing the quality, a handful of saffron from a blue monkey which has taken it from a shallow basket at her feet. Behind the woman, on her right, is a winged griffin, tied to a square loop on the wall with a leash round its neck. Clearly her status is exceptional, if not divine, and she has been named the 'Mistress of the Animals'. To her left, beyond the monkey, is another girl with short curly hair and tiered skirt pouring the contents of her full basket into a large overflowing basket on the floor. The connecting theme of this composition is the saffron crocus: it appears in the background; it is collected; it decorates the silk top and braiding of the larger woman's bodice; she even has two crocus stamens tattooed on her cheek. Clearly this valuable commodity played an important part in ritual in the Bronze

Age, as well as being used as a dye for food or clothing.

The second of the upper rooms seems to be decorated on two walls with three older women wearing their hair in snoods, and with a scene of reeds and ducks. The relationship of these to the main area is as yet unknown.

Costume

These wall-paintings provide a great deal of information about the clothes that were worn by, or familiar to, the Mycenaeans. It is not clear whether it is their best rather than their everyday dress which is depicted or even, in some cases, an archaic ceremonial costume, however unlikely this may seem. No actual garments survive to assist with this, and no other styles are illustrated, but there are other sources of information such as figurines, gold rings, sealstones and carved ivories. Few connections can be made with the descriptions of clothing in the later epic poetry, and it is dubious whether even these have any validity. Homer's descriptions are formulaic and unspecific with reference to elaborate decoration or rich materials, which probably reflect contemporary rather than Bronze Age costume. The precise meaning of the few terms he does use, *chiton, pharos* and *chlaina*, is unknown.

The textiles available to the Bronze Age people of the Aegean were made of wool from both sheep and goats, of linen and, to a limited degree, of silk. The recent discovery of the cocoon of a variety of silk moth at Akrotiri and the transparency of some of the fabrics painted on the frescoes there suggest that silk was available, if only as a luxury. In the Classical period silk cloth was regularly imported as a luxury from the East; Aristotle also reports sericulture on the island of Cos using the cocoon of a native moth, long before the introduction of the 'Chinese' silk moth (*Bombyx mori*) which became the basis of Mediterranean production from the Byzantine period. This 'wild silk' needs to be spun, unlike cultivated silk which can be reeled from the cocoon in a single filament. True cotton does not seem to have been cultivated in Greece until the 5th century BC, although there is a native cotton whose threads are too weak to make cloth and would only be suitable for embroidery. The whorls necessary for hand-spinning of all these fibres are found in a large variety of materials throughout the Bronze Age Aegean.

The frescoes show that many fabrics were patterned and colourful. Natural colours could be obtained from undyed wool (black, white and brown) or a variety of plants (leaves, flowers, roots or bark), lichens, insects, shellfish and coloured earths were all used to prepare dyes of many shades. For example, saffron or onion skins could be used for yellow, madder or the eggs of the kermes (coccus) insect for red, indigo for blue, and the dye sac from the murex shell for purple. Most vegetable dyes need a *mordant* to fix the colour and prevent it fading or washing out, such as vinegar, salt or urine which were readily available. No dye-works have been recognised in excavation but, given the centralised control of the palaces over all aspects of cloth production, such an area may yet be discovered. Large vats in clay and cauldrons in copper exist in plenty. Either would be adequate for use in dyeing.

The Linear B tablets, particularly from Pylos, are very specific with reference to the different qualities of cloth and the processes of production. These were shared out in a way which resembles mediaeval practice. Carders, spinners, dyers and weavers were all separate 'trades'. Towns or villages specialised in the production of certain types of cloth and presumably were well known for this. Some workers are recorded as drawing rations from the palace. Whether they were free or slaves is not certain but presumably both were employed in such a major industry. The image conjured up by Homer of a working woman weighing out wool to ensure a meagre ration of food for her children (*Iliad* XII, 433-435) in order to describe a battle hanging in the balance, is not only a simile charged with an extraordinary range of symbolism, but also a vivid reminder of Bronze Age practices.

The style of clothing worn makes the most economical use of cloth woven on a narrow loom without resorting to wasteful cutting or tailoring. The clay loomweights from upright warp-weighted looms of this kind are a common find outside the palaces. If weaving was also a palace activity, then a different kind of loom may have been in use of which no trace survives. This could have been a more sophisticated upright loom weighted with a wooden beam or roller rather than loomweights as known from Egypt at this period. Small hand or tapestry looms may also have been used but no trace survives. Interestingly, all the illustrations of looms in the Classical period, including those of Penelope at work, show a warp-weighted loom.

It would be suprising not to find some changes in the dress worn by **Women** over a period of some three-and-a-half centuries, but from the earliest depictions on the gold rings from the Shaft Graves and from the chamber tombs at Mycenae, where the medium allows limited detail, to the latest representations on the wall-paintings of the 13th century, the most characteristic dress of women is the tiered wrap-over skirt, already described, at Akrotiri. It varies from a short knee-length version seen at Akrotiri in the 'House of the Ladies' showing much of the underskirt, to a longer one of ankle length, as seen in the Room with the Fresco at Mycenae (Fig. 34, p. 111) and restored in the processional scenes from Tiryns and Thebes. In the House of the Ladies, one woman wears a skirt with tiers of a flimsy, crinkled material while a heavily pleated version can be found on the skirts of the Ivory Trio from Mycenae (Fig. 24, p. 79). The material from which they were made varied from a simple plain fabric, embellished with coloured bands as in the House of the Ladies and in the Room with the Fresco at Mycenae, to ones with an extremely complex weave as seen on the women in Xeste 3. The seated figure with cut foot in Xeste 3 at first sight looks different, yet also wears a basic wrap-over skirt decorated with loose hanging ribbons in groups of three in place of the usual pleats. Fringes are to be seen in the fringed warp-ends of the fabric on two skirts shown in the House of the Ladies. Most wrap-over skirts were tied round the waist with a cord but some may also have had a separate belt. Unlike some of the Cretan representations, there is no sign that an apron formed part of the costume.

A tight short-sleeved bodice fastened under the bosom was worn with this wrap-over skirt. It is difficult to judge whether an undershirt was worn since, unless the figure is of a young girl, the nipples are always visible. Even in the case of the Mykenaia who has a saffron-coloured undershirt, the nipples are shown. These bodices of plain or patterned material are decorated with intricately woven braid down the seams and edging the front and neck. According to the Linear B tablets these braids were woven by specialists. At Akrotiri, in addition to the tight fitting bodices which were probably of wool, at least two of the women from Xeste 3 are shown wearing a diaphanous silk top, which is decorated with a variety of motifs such as crocus stamens. In these paintings the braid, running down the seam line of the bodices from the shoulder to the elbow, often terminated in a tassel or series of tassels.

The nature of the wrap-over skirt with its opening front requires an underskirt, although this does not always show. Where it can be seen, it was also elaborated with border bands, tucks, braid or pleating, and depicted in a variety of colours. Whether this underskirt was attached to the bodice or a separate undergarment, or whether other chemises or petticoats were worn are questions which cannot be answered. As to underwear, who knows? – since, unlike in Egypt, no laundry lists have survived.

These were not the only garments worn by women. The 'priestess' from the West House at Akrotiri is shown with a cloak worn over one shoulder, as is the small figure in the lower zone in the Room with the Fresco at Mycenae. It would seem that this garment is an addition to the usual dress, for in both cases a bodice of the familiar type is depicted with an undershirt as well. A long, single-piece robe is worn by the seated figure on the Tiryns ring, by the figurine in the hand from Mycenae and by some of the women on the Agia Triada sarcophagus. Here too can be seen two women and three men in an unusual skirt, possibly an ankle-length version of a loincloth, also found on sealstones. Some illustrations do not fall into any category: on an electrum ring from Mycenae a large woman wears either a short skirt and ankle bracelets or, less probably, trousers below a skirt. The so-called lamenting women on the larnax from Tanagra (resembling nothing more than a chorus line of belly dancers) wear what most resembles a cropped T-shirt above a wrap-over skirt. A shawl is shown on the Ivory Trio, shared between the two women, but surprisingly the numerous Mycenaean figurines provide little information about dress. One of the women from Xeste 3 throws a veil of diaphanous material around her head, perhaps in the manner of Calypso or Circe as described in identical formulae (*Odyssey* V, 230-232; X, 543- 545) – one of the few possible echoes of Bronze Age dress in the epic.

Only at Akrotiri are **Girls** separately depicted and generally they wear the same garments as the older women in a less elaborate form.

Children do not feature very much in the iconographic repertoire of Aegean art except again at Akrotiri, where they are mostly shown naked apart from a belt, as in the case of the boxers. The usual convention for skin colour, red for males and white for females, may not extend to children. The small attendant with the bowl in the male scene from Xeste 3 is painted in yellow-ochre. One of the pair of boxers who wears an earring only associated with women, as well as necklaces, bracelets and anklets of beads, has a much paler face. Was yellow the colour intended to denote children without regard for their sex? A small child, probably female, part of the Ivory Trio from Mycenae, wears a long wrapped-over piece of material held in place with a belt.

Male dress included the simple short-sleeved tunics worn by grooms and soldiers at several sites. A basic white tunic could either be linen or wool, bound on the seams with contrasting braid. Others wear coloured or spotted tunics. These could be a uniform, a ceremonial dress or a mark of status. The everyday clothing of some men could well have been a tunic, but of a more practical colour (Fig. 26c).

Another garment is an unpleated kilt, though it is uncertain whether this was worn by all men or just those of higher status. The simplest form, like the tunic, was white with or without a contrasting border, as illustrated at Pylos. The male robing scene from Xeste 3 shows a white linen loincloth and coloured woven kilt (Fig. 26b) which indicates that, as in Egypt, a loincloth was worn as underwear. Kilts of very similar

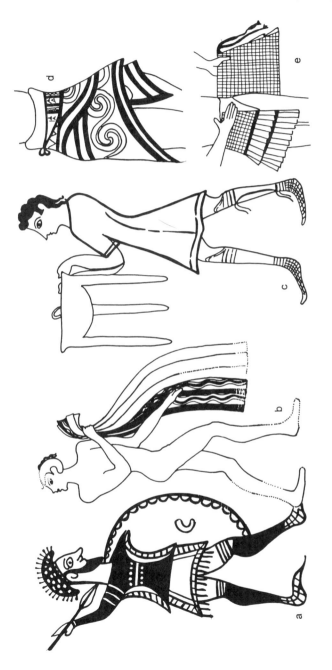

Fig. 26 a) Tunic with jerkin on Warrior Vase, c. 1150 BC; b) Xeste 3, c. 1500 BC, carrying kilt and ? loin cloth; c) tunic and greaves, tripod bearer from Pylos, c. 1230 BC; d) kilt, Xeste 4 c. 1500 BC, cf (b); e) diagram of kilt.

pattern are shown on the staircase procession in the neighbouring house, Xeste 4 (Fig. 26d, p. 89). The paintings in the tomb of Rekhmire in Egypt show one of the latest scenes depicting the Aegean tribute-bearers named *Keftiu* (Fig. 28, p. 95). The garment worn by these men was changed during the execution of the painting, from the white linen loincloth, popular in Crete, to a more intricately patterned woven kilt. This change may reflect the shift of power from Minoan Crete to the Mycenaean mainland during the 15th century – or may set right a sartorial solecism. It is usually said that a Cretan-style codpiece has been partly erased, but both here and on earlier paintings of Keftiu, this looks more like an empty sheath for a dagger, appropriate for a friendly embassy. The soldier drawn on the back of a Linear B tablet from Mycenae is also depicted wearing a kilt (Fig. 15, p. 46), while at Pylos, at least, a male wears one in the Cretan style, also seen at Akrotiri. The quaintly drawn soldiers on the Warrior Vase are shown with some kind of jerkin and fringed skirt (Fig. 26a, p. 89). A further style is worn by some of the fighting soldiers in the Pylos wall-paintings, who appear to have a black, possibly leather, skirt cut in points, worn as protection over a white undergarment, perhaps a white tunic.

There are men dressed in skins – perhaps illustrating barbarians or foreigners – but many males are just naked or in loincloths. Three varieties of loincloth can be seen in the Ship Fresco at Akrotiri. On the mainland some men of status are shown wearing a long ankle-length tunic, patterned or flounced, as is the Bard at Pylos. Obvious foreigners with dark or black skins are dressed no differently from those presumed to be Mycenaeans.

That all these varieties of garment may depict rank is suggested by the tablets from Knossos where, in the *wool* series, particular qualities of wool are specified as suitable for cloaks for the followers (*hequetai*). Many different types of cloaks are illustrated. On the painted vases charioteers appear to wear a cloak-like garment (Fig. 29d, p. 97). In the 'meeting on the hill' in the miniature wall-painting in the West House at Akrotiri, cloaks with a distinctive neckline are worn by the men and also by some of those seated in the ships. Interestingly, the lefthand female figure in the wall-painting from the Room with the Fresco at Mycenae wears a similar cloak. The greater detail of this particular cloak shows that it was woven with *flokati* (tufts) on the inside. Heavy, hairy cloaks are worn by men in the West House scenes. Which, if any, of these wearers are hequetai remains a puzzle.

Although most people will have gone barefoot for at least part of the time, leather mesh boots, as worn by the soldiers on the Warrior Vase, were probably widespread. Clay models exist of highly decorated knitted socks with leather base and pointed toes, similar to those worn by the Keftiu in the Rekhmire wall-painting.

Varieties of **hairstyle** may indicate age and/or status for both men and women. At Akrotiri, at least, a case can be made for three different age groups with different hairstyles. Young boys and girls have shaved heads with a pony-tail and the characteristic lock of hair above the forehead which remains throughout life (Fig. 26b, p. 89). As they near puberty, their hair is either allowed to grow and is depicted short and curly with the forelock and pony-tail (Fig. 27d, p. 92) or still partly shaven with several uncut locks. With maturity in women the head of hair is complete and long locks standard, elaborately bound with ribbons and beads. This is the style best known on the mainland, as seen in most of the processional frescoes. Other women are shown with their hair in a snood. Some mature men seem to have their hair short, worn with a fillet (band) in the case of the ivory head from Mycenae (Frontispiece); others retain the characteristic long locks.

Certain women, such as the small figure in the Room with the Fresco at Mycenae, the chariot-riders on the Agia Triada sarcophagus and the seated female on the Tiryns ring, are shown wearing a *polos* hat, usually with a plume. This hat can also be seen on many figurines, large and small (Fig. 25a, p. 83). The hat with a plume is a mark of distinction shared with sphinxes, such as the plaster head from Mycenae and those carved on the ivory pyxis from Thebes, and on plaques from Mycenae. Men are generally depicted bareheaded unless wearing helmets, with the exception of an Egyptianizing hood worn by some men at Pylos.

Most women are depicted wearing a wide variety of **jewellery** (Fig. 27, p. 92) from necklaces to bracelets, earrings, hairpins and sealstones at the wrist, as well as ankle-bracelets. The colours used and shapes represented accurately reflect actual examples found in graves and other contexts. The jewellery worn by the Mistress of the Animals in the Xeste 3 scene, for example, includes hoop earrings of gold, dragonfly and duck necklaces of gold and lapis lazuli or blue glass, gold discs stitched to the braid on the sleeve and papyrus-shaped blue beads at the wrist. All this jewellery can be paralleled in the Shaft Graves. While the antecedents of the culture at Akrotiri are naturally Cycladic, it is usually the Minoan connections of the wall-paintings and other features at Akrotiri which are sought for and stressed, to the extent that some claim it as a Minoan colony. The use of this fashion in jewellery, shared with those buried in the royal Shaft Graves at Mycenae, emphasises once again the essential unity of Aegean Late Bronze Age art and fashion, in the context of wider exchanges throughout the Eastern Mediterranean area.

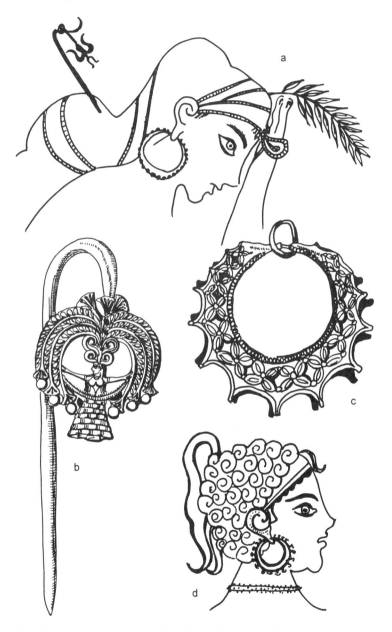

Fig. 27 Matching jewellery from Shaft Grave III (b & c) and Xeste 3 (a & d): hairpin, ht of dangle c. 7cm; earring, ht 9cm.

Chapter 10
Trade and contact

Resources and the sea

Greece is not an area rich in mineral resources. The agriculture of many areas is marginal, metal-bearing ores are limited and there are few other precious raw materials to be found. The geography of the country divides it into small units of fertile land separated by steep rugged mountains and each short distance overland was a major journey in the days before roads and railways. The prosperity and achievements of Greeks in the Mycenaean or Classical periods are almost inconceivable: if they had not happened they would be hard to imagine. There are, however, two assets which the inhabitants of this unpromising land have from time to time been able to harness to their own advantage. One is natural – the sea. The coastline is so indented that there are few parts of Greece far from a harbour or sheltered beach. The many islands of the Aegean provide stepping stones from one area to the next. As soon as seaworthy boats were developed – and this clearly happened long before the Mycenaean period – a long distance or a heavy load were no bar to contact. The second asset is human – a native ingenuity and curiosity well documented in the Classical period and, to judge by the extent of their trading contacts, fully exercised in the Mycenaean.

Maritime trade

The exploitation of these two assets allowed the Mycenaeans, and indeed the Minoans before them, to participate in the network of maritime trade long established along the coasts of the Eastern Mediterranean between the mouth of the Nile, the coasts of what today are Israel, Lebanon and Syria, Cyprus and the southern coast of Anatolia (home, by the Late Bronze Age, to the powerful Hittite civilization). From here the merchants of different nationalities, documented in the archives of these Near Eastern states, provided overland links with much more distant parts – Upper Egypt or Mesopotamia, for example. The same maritime trade allowed the Mycenaeans to reach out more and more to explore the resources of the central Mediterranean as far as Sardinia and even the head of the Adriatic sea. Mycenaean pottery serves as a marker for the extent of this trade, an extent which directly reflects the prosperity of Mycenaean civilization.

Sailing patterns

Although distance is no obstacle to maritime contact, the seafarer is at the mercy of wind and weather as may be learnt from the adventures of Odysseus, though these may well reflect a later period of exploration (Chapter 12). The sailing season is short, from late spring to early autumn, and the winds unpredictable. In the Aegean, the summer *meltemi* – a sudden, vicious, north wind – has sunk many a ship, even modern ones, unable to reach the shelter of a lee shore. Although stone anchors of similar pattern are known from the Black Sea to Egypt, the ancient preference, wherever possible, was for the safety of beaching ships – as the Achaeans did before Troy – rather than the perils of riding at anchor. Thus important Bronze Age sites are often close to shallow, sandy or gravelly beaches.

The pictures of boats on sealstones and in wall-paintings such as that in the West House at Akrotiri show us that galleys and sailing ships with steering oars were available to the Mycenaeans. The evidence from the cargo ships wrecked off Cape Gelidonya and Ulu Burun near Kaṣ, both on the most dangerous part of the southern Anatolian coast, show that they were quite small. The Kaṣ ship is estimated to have been 17m. long, the Gelidonya ship only 10m. The prevailing patterns of wind and currents make the direct crossing from Crete to the north coast of Africa relatively simple: Odysseus reports that it took five days to reach the Nile (*Odyssey* XIV, 255-257). From there the return journey had to be coastal to Cyprus or Syria, following the current that flows anticlockwise around the eastern end of the Mediterranean. The last and most perilous part of the journey – which the Gelidonya and Kaṣ ships failed to complete – was to a landfall in eastern Crete or Rhodes and the shelter of the familiar Aegean islands.

As can be discovered from the accounts of the great grain ships which later fed Rome with Egyptian wheat, it was unlikely that more than a single round trip would be completed in any sailing season by the time allowance had been made for frequent stops to barter the cargo or wait for a favourable wind. How many ships made this journey each year, or indeed whether the journey was made every year, is far from certain. The sum total of Mycenaean products found in the Near East, and Near Eastern products found in Greece over a period of nearly six hundred years, would hardly form the cargo of one small boat. Without the cargoes of the two wrecks mentioned, there would be little idea of the scale of this trade.

Trade and exchange

To call this activity 'trade' is perhaps misleading – though Hesiod has no hesitation in doing so for his father's unprofitable voyages in the 7th century BC. Many mechanisms are known which lead to the exchange and dispersal of goods over a wide area. One of the most familiar of these is the so-called 'gift exchange' reported by Homer. These include the gifts, for example, of the Phaeacian lords to the destitute Odysseus (*Odyssey* XIII), which were not immediately returned but made in the expectation that at some future date an equivalent gift would be made to keep the balance straight. The Near Eastern archives record gifts from one brother king to another, but also document in precise detail the rates of exchange for different commodities. Wall-paintings in Egyptian tombs from the 14th century BC (Fig. 28) show tributaries labelled Keftiu – perhaps the Egyptian word for Cretans – bringing offerings of precious metal vases characteristic of the Aegean area, as well as folded cloth;

Fig. 28 Keftiu in the wall-painting of the tomb of Rekhmire, 15th century BC. The right-hand figure carries an ox-hide ingot on his shoulder.

but, as far can be told, the people of the Aegean were never subject to Egyptian suzerainty. According to Homer, Agamemnon and Menelaus' men traded bronze, gleaming iron, hides, live cattle or slaves for wine from Lemnos (*Iliad* VII, 467-475). However the trade was described or carried out, there are clear signs that the Mycenaeans were partners in this trade, however sporadically. The weights and measures of the Aegean are often the same as those found in the Near East, while the copper ingot 'standard' – the 'ox-hide' ingot – has been found from Israel to Sardinia and is depicted in the same series of tomb-paintings in Egypt.

The Kaş and Gelidonya wrecks

The merchant ship which sank near Kaş around 1315 BC provides a vivid insight into the cargoes of the period, even though it is not certain where its home port may have been or whether it was heading for the Aegean. The bulk of the cargo was formed by hundreds of copper ox-hide ingots and dozens of the 'Canaanite' storage and transport jars (Fig. 29b) typical of the area of modern Israel. The contents of most of these did not survive, though many contained terebinth resin used in Egyptian burial rites for embalming or for the manufacture of perfume. Pottery vessels from Cyprus were packed in large pithoi for safe shipment. Other commodities in smaller quantity included ingots and scrap items of tin, ingots of glass, pieces of trimmed elephant and hippopotamus tusks and logs of 'Egyptian' ebony. Among the many items recovered, some precious trinkets may have belonged to the captain or a wealthy passenger. These include a unique and important gold scarab seal (Fig. 29c) with the royal name of Nefernefruaten Nefertiti, a gold chalice, pendants with Near Eastern motifs, and two cylinder seals, of which one is gold-mounted. Other precious metal items were already old or damaged at the time the ship sank, evidently collected as scrap metal. Large numbers of stone and bronze balance-weights were perhaps used for checking the exchange value of such items.

There were swords of Syrian and Mycenaean types as well as other weapons and tools. A few Mycenaean vases, including jugs and drinking cups, were surely for personal use, but these give no clue whether the captain and crew were Mycenaean or whether they just found them useful.

Perhaps the most intriguing find was a pair of recessed wooden tablets, well used and with a mended hinge (Fig. 29a). These were of exactly the kind which were filled with wax to provide a surface for writing – the ship's log, a traveller's diary or the 'accounts' for the voyage? The idea was known to Homer in the story of Bellerophon

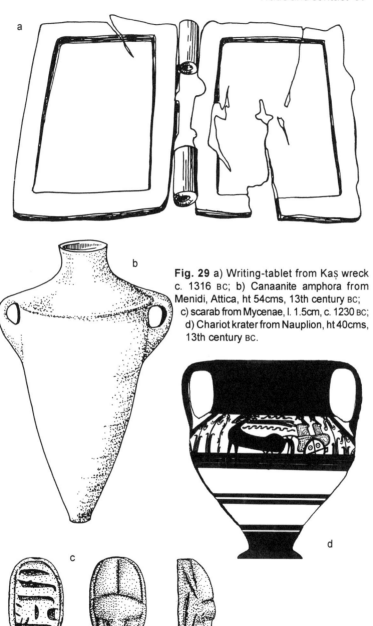

Fig. 29 a) Writing-tablet from Kaş wreck c. 1316 BC; b) Canaanite amphora from Menidi, Attica, ht 54cms, 13th century BC; c) scarab from Mycenae, l. 1.5cm, c. 1230 BC; d) Chariot krater from Nauplion, ht 40cms, 13th century BC.

taking a folded tablet to the king of Lycia, with instructions for his own death (*Iliad* VI, 202- 204). Otherwise, the earliest example of a wooden writing-tablet comes from 8th-century BC Nimrud in Assyria. Analysis of the residue on this tablet showed that the writing surface was formed of wax mixed with *orpiment* (a natural yellow mineral, arsenic trisulphide). One of the Canaanite amphorae on the wreck contained orpiment – though if it was intended for writing-tablets, it would supply a very great number. Overall, the wreck provides a familiar image of a coastal trading ship loading and offloading different cargoes, and investing in a range of commodities, without necessarily having a specific customer for each.

The Gelidonya wreck is of a smaller, later ship, sunk about 1225 BC. Less of her cargo is preserved and the finds present an image of a rather different kind of activity. The bulk of the cargo was also of ingots but the range of other goods is absent. Instead, there were numbers of scrap items of bronze, including agricultural tools such as hoes rarely discovered in excavation on land, together with finished items. This boat may have had a more specialised role, moving from port to port with the raw materials for bronzeworking, exchanging new finished items for scrap and other commodities, perhaps setting up a workshop from time to time, for the cargo is reported to have even included a stone anvil.

The metals trade

These glimpses of trade cannot, of course, convey the whole picture. Much remains speculation but something can be deduced from the pattern as a whole. As suggested by the Kaş wreck, one of the most important imports to Greece was copper. The quantities of bronzework represented by offerings in tombs, by weapons and armour and by the fittings of the palaces and other buildings, are far greater than could be supplied by the one major copper source in the Aegean, at Laurion in Attica. It may even be that the whole of this trade was driven by the need to acquire copper and tin from distant sources. The copper ores of Cyprus first, and then Sardinia, were exploited in the Mediterranean trade, but the pattern of exchange is complex. Lead-isotope analysis, the most reliable technique for 'fingerprinting' bronze and other metals, shows that there are as yet undiscovered sources and suggest that, like coals to Newcastle or 'owls' to Athens, Cypriot copper could end up in ingot form in Sardinia. The sources of tin still elude us: there is no viable source in the Mediterranean area, although small quantities have been found in the Taurus mountains of southern Anatolia. It is possible that it was brought from further afield, from northern Spain, from the Erzgebirge (Ore Mountains) of Central Europe or from Africa, but there is no certainty about the origin of the tin used in Greece or, for that matter, in the Near East.

Other metals were less vital to Mycenaean civilization, but gold was clearly prized as a luxury and may have been brought from Egypt, or the rivers of Central Macedonia, Mt Pangaion in Eastern Macedonia or Thasos, where rich sources are all known to have been exploited in the Archaic period. Lead and silver were, however, both available from a number of sources of which the most valuable was at Laurion. Since silver was prized by the Egyptians and in the Near East, the Mycenaeans could have used it in exchange for other valuables, but this has not yet been demonstrated.

Luxury goods

Other materials imported to Greece were chiefly luxuries: elephant ivory from Syria or East Africa; hippopotamus ivory from the Nile; ostrich eggshells from North Africa; lapis lazuli from Syria, but ultimately from Afghanistan; amber from the Baltic coast or north Germany, brought by trade to the head of the Adriatic or, less probably, to the mouth of the Danube; glass in ingot form; resin and other substances in the Canaanite jars already mentioned. Finished goods were much rarer: vases of faience (much favoured by the Egyptians); occasional stone vases from Egypt or clay pots from Cyprus; trinkets such as faience scarab seals from Egypt, stone cylinder seals from Mesopotamia or Cyprus, and amulets of various materials. One extraordinary group of 38 carved Mesopotamian cylinder seals, spanning nearly a thousand years, was found in the palace treasury room at Thebes. There were also another 26 uncarved examples. Most, carved and uncarved, were of lapis lazuli. It would be nice to think that the examples found in the Kaş wreck were intended for this collection, evidence for one of the earliest antiquaries in Europe. Other goods were surely imported but most have left no trace. Together with these goods will have come ideas: of business practices and adminstration, of technology and design, of art and religion.

Perfume trade?

This trade, whether in materials, finished goods or ideas, cannot have been one way, but it is much harder to see what the Mycenaeans or their Minoan predecessors had to offer in exchange. Most of the Mycenaean pottery found beyond Cyprus is in the form of containers, usually small vases of no particular value. These either have constricted necks to hold precious liquids (stirrup jars) or wider necks for a more solid commodity, and it was presumably the contents rather than the containers that found a ready market in the Near East and Egypt. The decoration on the containers, like wine labels today, may have helped 'foreign' customers to identify the contents of each. At least in the areas administered by the palaces, olive oil was widely available, and frequent references on the clay tablets at Pylos and Mycenae to aromatic substances and oil-boilers suggest a perfume and ointment industry on quite a large scale. The terebinth resin already mentioned in the Kaş wreck may well have been destined for one of these Mycenaean manufactories.

Within Greece in the 13th century BC there is much evidence for the production of olive oil surpluses in such areas as central and western Crete. These were shipped in large stirrup jars painted before they were fired with 'codes' in Linear-B script (Fig. 30). Whether these gave the place of origin or describe some particular characteristic, they suggest sophisticated organisation. Jars of this kind have been found – presumably where their contents were wanted – in Thebes and in Attica, and at the House of the Oil Merchant outside the citadel at Mycenae, where some still had their seals intact (Fig. 30) when this building was destroyed by fire, as well as at many other sites.

Chariot kraters

At least one class of pottery was exported for its own sake. Large kraters (wine mixing-bowls) were decorated in the late 14th and early 13th centuries BC with scenes of horses with chariots (Fig. 29, p. 97), or of bulls and other animals, in a simple, attractive style. These were popular in Cyprus, where they were often placed in graves, and have been found as far inland as Amman in modern Jordan.

Cloth

Another traded product, of which little survives, is cloth. The ceilings of some Egyptian tombs were covered with paintings, perhaps of Aegean textiles, and folded cloth appears in the tribute of the Keftiu. At Pylos and especially at 'Mycenaean' Knossos there were enormous flocks of sheep under palace control listed on the Linear B tablets, and there are references to textiles of various types, often with untranslatable descriptions, as well as wool and linen. Trade may have been in the finished product rather than raw wool. Some items mentioned may well have been dyestuffs which might help to explain the popularity of the murex shell –

Fig. 30 a) Oil jar with Linear B symbol, Thebes, ht c. 45cm; b) Linear B tablet, Knossos, showing record of at least 1800 of these stirrup jars; c) jar with stopper in place, ht 37cms; d) stopper with seal impressions, House of Oil Merchant, Mycenae; e) onyx seals, Mycenae Chamber Tomb 515, with wounded lion ('the lion playing marbles'), diam. 2.3cm and cow with calf, diam. 2.4cm.

well known as a source of purple dye – as a decorative motif on Mycenaean pottery.

Manpower

Another likely commodity in Mycenaean trade is manpower. Homer reports the fate of sacked cities and the taking of slaves, especially women. The tablets make frequent reference to male and female slaves, some described as captives. Raids like those described in the epics were perhaps a feature of Mycenaean life, and they had no difficulty in obtaining slaves to exchange for goods in the markets of the Near East. Slavery was a common practice in the Near East at this time. A second form of manpower which is possible, but undocumented, could have been mercenary soldiers. Did Mycenaean warriors, like those of Classical Greece, provide hardier military forces than many locally available in the Eastern Mediterranean?

Cyprus

From the beginning of the Late Bronze Age Cyprus, with its rich copper sources, had a special position in trade with the Aegean. Mycenaean pottery becomes more and more frequent there. Some settlement on the island by Mycenaean Greeks took place as early as the 13th century BC. With the collapse of Eastern Mediterranean trade and the Mycenaean palaces almost simultaneously, c. 1200 BC, it seems that Mycenaean influence in Cyprus suddenly became much stronger. Chamber tombs replaced earlier types and Mycenaean pottery was made locally. This is perhaps the most likely period for the Greek population, present in the Archaic era, to have become established on the island. Opinion differs as to whether these settlers were refugees from the destructions in the mainland, or whether they were in some way part of the wave of Sea Peoples which caused such havoc at this time further east. Whatever the cause, relations between Greece and Cyprus remain relatively strong, even when most signs of contact further east disappear for nearly three centuries.

Macedonia and the Black Sea

Although contact with Troy was already established at the beginning of the Mycenaean period, the extent of any Mycenaean trade into the Black Sea remains uncertain, even if the legend of the Golden Fleece and the voyage of the Argo reflect Bronze Age reality. On the northern coast of the Aegean, Mycenaean pottery reached Central Macedonia from the 15th century BC and became more and more common until the 12th century BC, but the local character of Macedonian culture remained largely unchanged. Several of the rivers 'ran with gold' in the Archaic period (and until recently) and may have supplied the Mycenaeans. Mycenaean weapons were prized in Albania and the Danube valley in the early Mycenaean period. Rapiers and local imitations of them are widely, if thinly, distributed, but by the palatial period this trade has ceased and the typical Mycenaean short sword of the 13th century BC is found beyond the Mycenaean area only in Epirus. Several metal types, both weapons and ornaments, which appear in Greece towards the end of the Mycenaean period, have parallels in Central Europe or northern Italy, and perhaps became known through the Adriatic trade that continued to bring amber to Greece until the end of the Bronze Age.

Italy and the Central Mediterranean

Apart from the copper and amber already mentioned, Italy and the Central Mediterranean had little to offer the Mycenaeans, or at least what they had does not survive. The Mycenaean pottery found in Sicily and in southern Italy exhibits the full range of types: containers, bowls and drinking vessels. There is no particular emphasis on a perfume trade and some of the pottery appears to have been made locally. This may indicate that the Mycenaean interest in this area was as much in acquiring land and planting colonies as in trade. The earliest examples of olive stones in Italy, from Broglio di Trebisacce in eastern Calabria, which date to the 13th century BC, suggest the introduction of Mycenaean farming practices. Few sites have yet been reported sufficiently to assess the proportion of Mycenaean to local Italian pottery and thus to estimate, in the roughest way, how 'Mycenaean' they were. Mycenaean pottery is well represented in Sardinia and sherds have been reported in both the Po Valley in northern Italy and in Spain. New research and new discoveries continually add to this picture of trade in the central and western Mediterranean.

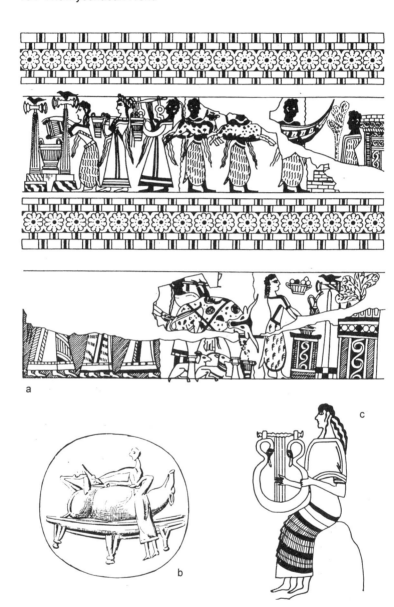

Fig. 31 a) Painted stone sarcophagus from Agia Triada, Crete, l. 1.37m, c. 1400 BC, see page 107; b) agate sealstone from Chamber Tomb 47 at Mycenae with sacrificial boar on table, diam. 2.2cm; c) the 'Bard' from Pylos with lyre, ht c. 34cms. c. 1250 BC.

Chapter 11
Religion

In the *Iliad* and in the *Odyssey* the gods play a leading role in the affairs of men. Indeed, as has often been remarked, Homer's men behave like gods and the gods like men. How far these Olympian gods are the same as those feared and venerated in the Bronze Age is a vexed question. While the Greeks were still thought of as newcomers after the end of the Bronze Age, it was easy to assume that their gods were also newcomers, and that some trace of their usurpation of an older generation is preserved in the legends of Kronos and Rhea. Now that the Linear B tablets can be read, it is sure that divinities with at least the same names, if not the same characteristics, were worshipped in the Mycenaean period. The names of Zeus and Hera, Poseidon and Athena, Hermes and Hephaistos, can all be recognised among others, while familiar titles such as *Potnia* (Mistress, in Classical Greece regularly applied to Demeter) also occur.

Without literature or written history from this period, very little can be known directly about the importance of these gods and goddesses. In the tablets, they seem to hold land just as in later periods, and have servants, while one tablet appears to be a record of offerings made to one of the gods. Beyond this level we must look for the material remains of shrine buildings, cult objects, burial practices or the depictions of religious activity in art. In studying these mute traces of ancient beliefs it must be recognised that here, more than in any other aspect of Greek prehistoric civilization, care must be taken not to impose our own ideas, or those appropriate to other times and places, on the evidence which survives. The anthropologist can observe living examples of cult practices, including the manipulation of expressive action, vocal utterances or symbolic objects. In contrast, the archaeologist is all too often restricted to the examination of the surviving paraphernalia of that which is believed to reflect religious activity, as a basis for inference about their use or symbolic meaning. Any closer approach to the underlying beliefs can only be speculative.

It is likely that there were many divinities, often with local characteristics and attributes, and that cult practices varied from place to place even when the same god or goddess was worshipped. Elements borrowed from the beliefs and practices of the Near Eastern and Egyptian societies, with whom trade brought them into contact, may also be expected, just as happened extensively in later periods. It is to this source that the Mycenaeans probably owed mythical creatures such as the griffin or the sphinx which often seem to have religious associations in Mycenaean art.

Inevitably in the search for temples and household cult, for the evidence of sacrifice and other offerings, or for the existence of specific rituals and objects of veneration, criteria derived from other areas or periods must be employed. These criteria may be based on well-documented religious complexes and structures of distinctive character and used to help identify places or objects connected with the practice of cult or ritual.

The identification of scenes in wall-painting, or of specific buildings and groups of objects as religious, should result from the cumulative process of assembling a variety of evidence. Identification relies on the combination of a number of special features, which cannot easily be explained as domestic, functional or purely decorative. Relevant features of this kind include the unusual location of a building, whether actual or depicted in a scene, and the presence of distinctive architectural features. The combination of location and character may suggest either, at one extreme, provision for public display or, at the other, for hidden mysteries. Special facilities such as platforms and attention-focussing devices, of which the most obvious might be a figure or wall-painting placed in a prominent position, indicate a special function. Unusual equipment, such as axes, stands or model horns, which do not seem to have a practical function, reinforce the impression of cult use, while groups of figurines, jewellery and other objects which seem out of place in domestic contexts may represent durable offerings. Often the members of a community may take exceptional pains to honour or placate their divinities, vying with each other to provide the most ostentatious or valuable offerings (though it must always be remembered that perceived value differs from one society to another). Unlike the Greeks of the Classical period, however, the Mycenaeans do not appear to have devoted their resources to the construction of elaborate 'temple' buildings. In addition, there are often everyday objects such as cooking, storage and drinking vessels which played some role in the communal celebrations – drinking or feasting – that are so universally a feature of cult activity.

Once any complex assemblage of features has been judged religious in character, then individual elements, when recognised elsewhere, may also be interpreted as indicating religious significance, especially where unnecessary repetition is observed. Certain items may have been charged with a symbolism which was recognisable whether they were used in an overtly sacred or purely domestic context. Here, however, even greater caution is required since objects of similar type have both sacred and secular functions and the same objects serve as both sacred and secular at different times. There is not space in the account that follows to justify each of the interpretations we have presented. We have exercised caution, which some may feel excessive. Others will find even this level of interpretation too subjective. We shall have succeeded in our aim, if readers are able to understand the range of information which has been used as the foundation for religious interpretation and are prepared to criticise it rigorously and sceptically.

Religious scenes

A large number of illustrations of activity, interpreted as religious, survive from the Late Bronze Age in different ways – wall-paintings, scenes carved on gold rings or sealstones, or painted on larnakes (stone or clay coffins). This is an area in which it is hard to separate Minoan and Mycenaean or to know whether Minoan scenes in Mycenaean contexts had the same significance for those whose saw them.

The well-preserved cult scene from Xeste 3 at Akrotiri has already been described (Chapter 9), while the most complete scene which survives to illustrate cult at this period is painted in miniature on the stone larnax from a tomb at Agia Triada in Crete (Fig. 31, p. 104). This dates to the period immediately after the destruction of the Minoan palaces. On one long side, divided into three zones, are shown two groups, men and women, moving in opposite directions. The men carry two animals, perhaps calves, and what seems to be a model boat, towards a standing figure in front of a small building with a tree beside it. This is variously interpreted as a divinity in front of a shrine or as the dead man standing in front of his tomb. The figure is smaller than the others and often reconstructed without feet, leading to the suggestion that it is a statue. One of the women carries a yoke with a pair of large buckets across her shoulders, while the other pours from a similar bucket into a large vessel set between a pair of stands with double-axes on top of them. Birds perch on the axes. The women are accompanied by a man playing a lyre.

On the opposite side is shown a scene of sacrifice – ritual slaughter. A spotted ox lies bound on an elaborate table or altar. Its throat cut, the blood runs into a bucket similar to those on the other side of the sarcophagus. Below the table two goats appear to await their fate, while behind it a man plays a double pipe. To the left, a woman (white feet) places her hands on the bull in what is surely a ritual gesture, while beyond her are two pairs

Fig. 32 Daemons: a) gold ring, Tiryns Treasure, l. 5.6cm; b) wall-painting, Cult Centre at Mycenae, ht 8.5; c) glass plaque, Mycenae, ht 3cm; d) Sealstone, Vapheio, diam. 1.8cm.

of women bystanders (?). On the right, perhaps in a separate scene denoted by the change in the background colour, another woman places her hands in a similar gesture on a low table, or altar. Behind her in the same zone possibly hanging on the wall, are a jug and a basket of fruit or bread. Another double-axe with a perching bird stands on the floor behind the altar. Beyond this is a building with 'horned' decoration on its roof and a tree growing inside it. Is this the depiction of a shrine or sanctuary?

On one end of the larnax, a pair of women ride in a horse-drawn chariot. On the other end, the women, again in a chariot, wear elaborate head-dresses and are drawn by winged griffins. A bird flutters in the background. The contrast is presumably intentional. Do the figures represent human and divine or, in the context of burial, the present life and the afterlife?

It is not known whether these scenes are specific to burial rituals or whether they are of wider significance. Even so a number of elements can be detected that seem to be associated with cult, which may help us to identify it in less complex pictures. There is the custom of animal *sacrifice* (Fig. 31b, p. 104) – not just wasteful slaughter but a prelude to a communal feast – carried out with specific rites, much as today the animals for Jewish or Moslem consumption are slaughtered in accordance with specific religious prescriptions. Homer makes it plain that the gods only receive a portion of an animal, burnt on the sacrificial fire, while the celebrants enjoy all the choicest parts (*Iliad* II, 402-431, *Odyssey* III, 454-463). Offerings of the produce of the land, or of the blood of the slaughtered animals, at shrines or altars, are no different from the regular practices at Classical Greek sanctuaries, and appear to be normal Mycenaean practices. Shrines and altars, depicted with *horns of consecration* (carved stone or wooden horns perhaps intended to represent, schematically, bull's horns), trees or double-axes, are characteristic of many scenes. The male and female figures which are often placed in focal positions may or may not represent the presence of a god or goddess.

Strange creatures, usually termed Daemons, with leonine muzzles and paws, and scaly 'wing-cases' are frequently illustrated (Fig. 32). A procession of them on the large gold ring from Tiryns (Fig. 32a) carry round-bodied long-necked jugs towards a female figure seated on a folding chair with a footstool who holds up a chalice ready to receive their libations. She wears a head-dress and is accompanied by a hawk – symbols which may indicate she is a goddess rather than a priestess. Ears of wheat between the creatures and in the upper border are a reminder of the importance of cereal crops, perhaps even of the role of Demeter, while the sun and crescent moon are also depicted.

The 'great goddess' ring from Mycenae (Fig. 33), found with a hoard of precious objects near Grave Circle A, has a scene possibly set in the countryside. This also depicts a female – goddess or priestess – seated under a tree, either giving or receiving a bunch of poppy heads. She is flanked by two small dumpy females (dwarfs or twins?). On the left another woman in a flounced skirt holds a bunch of lilies in her left hand and other flowers in her right. The final destination of these flowers is uncertain. In the central background is an upright double-axe. In the upper left an enigmatic figure is to be seen – a figure-of-eight shield with head and legs, arms and a sword! (A sentry on guard or an approaching god?) The sun and moon are shown above as are six heads on the left, serving to emphasise the impossibility of understanding their meaning today.

Fig. 33 Gold rings from Mycenae c. 1500 BC; a) from Chamber Tomb, c. 3cm. This enigmatic scene may represent the enforced separation of a man and a woman or a frenzied ritual at a rural sanctuary; b) The 'great goddess' ring from the Acropolis Treasure, l. 3.4cm. Both are drawn from impressions.

Fragments of wall-painting showing processions of offering are preserved from all the principal Mycenaean sites (Chapter 9), although it is not known whether these commemorated secular offerings to a ruler or cult offerings to a god. A scene of offering (Fig. 34) was found on the wall within one of the shrines at Mycenae, and here its symbolism is surely religious. Parts of three painted figures survive in the corner of the Room with the Fresco. A three-dimensional plastered and painted altar is set in the corner of the room and on the wall beside this to the left is a female figure, one-quarter life-size, holding up ears of wheat. She is accompanied by an animal, possibly a lion (suggested by the yellow colour), but this is barely preserved. On the wall above the altar, two female figures, at two-thirds life-size, face each other. The figure on the left is distinguished by a long cloak and holds the hilt of a sword. Facing her is another slightly smaller figure in a flounced skirt who holds out a staff, spear or a bow. Between them are two small male figures painted in solid colour, perhaps graffiti added later.

Fig. 34 Fresco from Mycenae c. 1250 BC. The head of the cloaked figure, the hilt of the sword and the type of the animal are conjectural. Restored drawing, original ht c. 1.90m.

Other scenes, perhaps set in the countryside, on several of the gold rings from the chamber tombs at Mycenae and elsewhere seem to depict different kinds of ritual, some static, some active. Men and women appear together, though the prominent position is almost always given to a woman. Mythical creatures, such as griffins and sphinxes, are also shown and sometimes accompany a female figure seated on a throne. Shrines with trees growing out of them are regularly depicted and in some cases men or women clasp them (Fig. 33a, p. 110). From Knossos comes a ring on which what seems to be a circular dance is performed by four women in flounced skirts, and a tiny figure (or a boar's tusk helmet) can be seen in the background. This particular scene has suggested to some scholars the concept of an *epiphany*, where rituals are performed to summon a divinity and make him or her appear to mortal men. The shield-figure on the 'great goddess' ring just described is sometimes thought to have a similar meaning.

On many examples of rings and sealstones, male and female figures are accompanied by animals, real or mythical. These may reflect the practice frequent in Egypt where particular divinities have an animal form as well as a human one, or are accompanied or represented by a specific animal. Control of wild animals may also have been a sign of power, and scenes depicting a 'mistress of the animals' (as in Fig. 23, p. 74) remind us of the Babylonian goddess Ishtar or the archaic Greek depictions of Artemis the huntress.

Scenes of mourning or funerary ritual are to be found on the series of clay larnakes from Tanagra, where women appear to tear their hair and touch their foreheads in a gesture of lament. This gesture is also found on bronze figurines, usually thought to be Cretan, from Kambos in Laconia and from Tylissos to the west of Knossos. A woman with the same gesture can be seen on the Warrior Vase.

Although all these scenes give hints of what to look for on the sites themselves, major problems remain as bars to interpretation. Some, like the Mycenae fresco, are placed in rooms where cult use is certain and are therefore directly connected to the function of the room itself. Others, such as the elaborately decorated rings, are thought to be the symbols of priestly authority and therefore related to the role or duty of the priests or priestesses who wore them. Others may only be decorative representations of well known stories, perhaps reflecting a Bronze Age mythology inaccessible to us – unless it is assumed that the myths of Classical Greece are the myths, or even the realities, of their distant ancestors.

Shrines

One architectural form of shrine is known to us from Bronze Age Greece, the 'tripartite shrine' with three rooms side by side. This is depicted on gold plaques from Shaft Graves III and IV at Mycenae, where birds perch on horns of consecration and other horns decorate the façade, on a similar plaque from Thessaly and in fragments of a miniature wall-painting from Knossos. One building of this form has been discovered, in Crete at Anemospelia near Archanes, where, exceptionally, a human sacrifice may have been taking place at the moment of destruction.

Those Mycenaean shrines that have been found are usually recog- nised by their contents rather than their form, though most have benches or platforms along their inner walls which may be the equivalent of the altars seen in the depictions. Failing any other explanation (and archae- ologists are often too eager to find shrines to seek for an alternative explanation), a collection of strange figurines and other objects is likely to indicate a cult room or area. So far, although many shrines have been claimed, there are only a few in the Mycenaean area where this interpre- tation would be hard to dispute. Two of these buildings are at Mycenae and date to the palatial period. Another of similar date has recently been found on Methana, while shrines used in the late Mycenaean period have been found at Tiryns and Phylakopi on Melos.

Two separate sanctuaries, built on the western slope at Mycenae before the citadel was extended, contain a large amount of cult material. These and the other buildings in this area have, in consequence, been named the 'Cult Centre'. Doubtless there were other more important sanctuaries within the citadel since these are architecturally undistin- guished and crowded into a small space between earlier buildings.

The Room with the Fresco complex consisted of a main room – with the fresco described previously – an inner shrine-cum-storeroom and two other rooms. The main room had a curiously constructed central hearth and an altar in the corner beside the doorway leading to the inner shrine. The equipment in the main room included a clay bath-tub, a lead vessel containing a range of objects (of which the most surprising was a faience plaque of Egyptian origin) and a variety of different types of pottery – a total of 47 storage jars and drinking vessels. Two outstanding ivory objects may be more directly related to the cult. An ivory head of a youth 6.8 cm high (see frontispiece) lay on the floor in front of the altar and could have formed part of a one-third life-size cult statue with a clothed wooden body. Close by was a couchant lion with a rectangular cut-out in its belly which shows that it was once an arm-rest for a throne or similar piece of furniture. Other objects suggested that some of the offerings were recycled by the priests. A good example of this is a pair of ivory hilt plates which had once decorated a bronze sword. One rivet was still in place to show that they had been cut off a weapon which had presumably either been refitted or melted down. The small inner shrine also had a slight bench at its rear on which stood an elegant, though damaged, female clay figure; another 24 pottery vessels were found in this room. All these objects had been left scattered on the floor after a minor catastrophe, perhaps an earthquake, had damaged the complex, and were then deliberately covered over, perhaps because they were, in some sense, sacred.

The second group of rooms, the Temple (Fig. 35), separated from the first by a passageway and approached from a completely different direction, consisted of an anteroom and a main room with a central platform or hearth and a series of benches at different levels around the rear. Originally there had been a storeroom behind this at a higher level, reached by a set of stairs, and an alcove where the rock was exposed. After the same disaster which ended the cult use of the Room with the Fresco, and during which much of the cult equipment of the Temple was broken, the fragments were sealed up in the storeroom and alcove and worship continued in the Temple alone. The only cult objects surviving in this phase were a severe figure (Fig. 36c, p. 117) and a broken clay offering-table on a bench in the rear corner of the room, almost out of sight behind one of the wooden columns which supported the roof. The objects from the earlier destruction are so far unparalleled. They included twenty-seven large, forbidding, male and female figures with arms raised, or holding implements, more than fifteen coiled clay snakes (Fig. 36a), a single small elegant figure (Fig. 36b) and three clay offering-tables. A clay bowl contained a selection of glass beads, and there was also a wide range of pottery vessels. It is improbable that the large figures represent divinities and they are more likely to be permanent representations of worshippers. Nearby another building, Tsountas' House, excavated in the 1890s, probably also contained a shrine. One room had a central hearth or altar of curious form and, beside it, a drain hole to take away libations or other liquid to a vessel at the edge of the room. Unlike the Room with the Fresco and the Temple, no unusual finds were made here.

At Phylakopi on the island of Melos, the two 12th-century BC cult rooms had some of the same features as at Mycenae. One unusual feature was a large boulder outside the entrance, perhaps a *baetyl* (cult stone) as shown on some of the gold rings. The range of finds, however, was different from that at Mycenae. There was one elegant female – with a painted beard! – but there were also roughly-modelled naked male figures and several cows with wheel-turned bodies and legs, a bronze figurine of Near Eastern type – a 'smiting god' with right arm raised – and, intriguingly, a sheet-gold face mask for a figurine of perishable material which has not survived. At Tiryns, the shrine consisted of a small room with a shallow porch, built against the wall of the lower citadel. At the back of the main room was a bench from which two female figures had fallen to the floor. Around the entrance to the shrine were found an unusual number of the small female and animal clay figurines which are well known in Mycenaean settlements and graves, but here, presumably, played a special role in the cult.

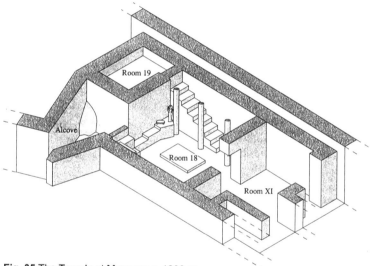

Fig. 35 The Temple at Mycenae c. 1200 BC.

The most recent discovery of a shrine – in Methana on the southwest coast of the Saronic gulf – shows how different the nature of the cult equipment can be in different places. Here a complex of rooms, still not fully explored, included one with a rough stone bench along the side wall. On this had once stood several models of horses and chariots, of 'driven' oxen and numerous individual model animals.

The frequent small female and animal Mycenaean figurines which have been found in early levels at Greek sanctuary sites, such as the temple of Aphaia on Aegina, Amyklae, and the temple of Athena at Delphi, suggest the possibility that some Mycenaean sanctuaries continued to be places of worship until the Archaic period and beyond.

Unlike Classical temples or Christian churches, none of the shrines found within Mycenaean sites is architecturally very impressive or placed in a particularly prominent position. They may only have been of secondary importance, used by limited groups within each community. The principal place of worship may have been within the palaces themselves, perhaps in the main room of the megaron, if the 'king' was also 'priest', officiating in 'public' ceremonies. Archaic Greek religion, however, at first took place in the open air with no more than an altar at which to dedicate offerings to the gods. Elaborately built shrines may be the exception rather than the rule. There is nothing about the shrine buildings depicted on the rings already described to indicate whether they are permanent stone structures, or temporary wooden ones which would leave little trace. The rural setting of some shrines depicted would, in any case, make it difficult to locate them archaeologically.

Figurines and cult equipment

Many examples of the small female and animal figurines already mentioned are found in domestic contexts as well as in tombs and cult places. Not all need have had cult significance and some could have been playthings, as suggested by their presence in children's graves. Model beds, tables and chairs are also well known. It is possible that each house had its own household shrine in which these played some role, but clearly they were not particularly revered since they are so frequently found in rubbish deposits. Larger figurines of clay, both elegant females and wheel-made animals, are much rarer. Occasionally larger heads of clay or stucco (such as the sphinx head from Mycenae) are found which, like the ivory head from Mycenae, must have belonged to some form of composite statue.

Other recognisable items of cult equipment are much rarer than in Crete where a wide range was in use and, of course, only those which were made of durable materials survive. Numerous items of wood or cloth may also have been present in the shrines and sanctuaries. Many early Archaic cult statues, for example, were wooden *xoana* (images of a deity) which are only known from literary references. There is little, apart from the ivory head from the Room with the Fresco, to show whether these were in use or not in the Mycenaean period. Elaborate rhyta of stone, in the form of bulls' heads, of metal, like the gold lion's head and the silver bull's head from the Shaft Graves, of faience, like a ram's head from the Kaṣ wreck, or of clay like a vessel decorated with three stags' heads from Volimidia near Pylos, are perhaps the most notable. Simpler clay funnels, however, were common and may have

Fig. 36 Clay figures from the Temple at Mycenae: a) Room 19, dia. 30cm; b) Room 19, ht 29cm; c) from platform in Room 18, ht 56cm.

served both cult and domestic purposes (as indeed could ordinary pots with holes drilled in their bases). Small clay tables with three short legs could, of course, have been for everyday use but are also found in cult contexts. Occasionally fragments of horns of consecration are found, but these are far rarer than in Crete.

Little specific funerary equipment has been recognised other than larnakes. An exception to this are bowls from the late Mycenaean cemetery of Perati in Attica, with four small female figures set around the rim. Their hands were placed on their heads in that, by now, familiar gesture of lament.

Conclusion

What can be made of this variety of information from the scenes, the cult places and the objects themselves? Clearly there are different practices and traditions represented, and belief in a multiplicity of divinities is confirmed by the names on the Linear B tablets. Figurines of many different types play an important role. Did they represent the worshippers in the case of the humans? Did they substitute for or act as reminders of offerings in the case of the animals? Did they form some kind of tableau (like a nativity scene) recreating a particular event? Female images predominate but this does not necessarily mean that divinities were predominantly female. Few figures seem distinguished enough to represent the gods or goddesses themselves. It is only because the anthropomorphism of Classical Greece is familiar that we expect the same of the Bronze Age. Other cultures have other traditions of representation and the Greeks of later periods knew of *aniconic* images of their gods, where a tree or pillar was enough to symbolise a divinity.

Offerings seem to play an important part in the cult practices – much as the Greeks later would take out 'insurance policies' with their protectors or protectresses. In the Classical world, a gift made in advance or promised in arrears was thought to be enough to secure success and prosperity if the right rituals had been observed. In the Bronze Age, the fertility of the earth, of the animals and of the family were surely prime concerns to a people whose dependence on their own resources was total. So too, in the often arid climate of the Aegean, the propitiation of divinities who controlled the rain, without which even fertile land would fail, must have been essential. But this is inference, not deduction, from the remains they have left behind them. The study of Bronze Age religion on the basis of later Greek mythology and belief has contributed much to deforestation and little to certainty.

Chapter 12
Homer and the Dark Age: myth or memory?

The gap in knowledge about the period between the end of the Myce-naean civilization and the beginning of the Archaic period – the gap which lent credence both to the idea of new populations and to the concept of a Dark Age – has begun to be filled in many parts of Greece. Indeed, some of the most exciting finds of Greek prehistoric archaeology in the last twenty years belong to this period.

It is not possible to date the creation of the *Iliad* and the *Odyssey* with any accuracy but the broad consensus of opinion places the last major stages of composition in the late 8th or early 7th century BC. Any assess-ment of the relationship of the Homeric epic to Mycenaean civilization is incomplete without taking into account the character of Greek society during the five hundred year period during which the traditional oral poetry that led up to Homer's epics was transmitted or evolved. The oral tradition can be seen either as a product of the Mycenaean period or of the following Dark Age.

The background of both Mycenaean and Dark Age society against which the epics should be set can now be seen much more clearly. In fact the term 'Dark Age' is now a misnomer which we would like to abandon, but we have not thought of a satisfactory alternative. Even more important for the understanding of Classical Greece is the historical continuum which can now be traced backwards in time from the Archaic period to the destruction of the Mycenaean palaces and beyond. There were changes but these were gradual and cumulative, rather than abrupt and radical, for there is no discontinuity in the archaeological record. The only sudden, widespread change that can be seen in the material remains is the disappearance of the palaces and the administrative system they supported. There are no innovations in the material record, no new styles of pottery and no new forms of metalwork which compel belief in the arrival of any large group in southern Greece at the end of the 13th century BC or later.

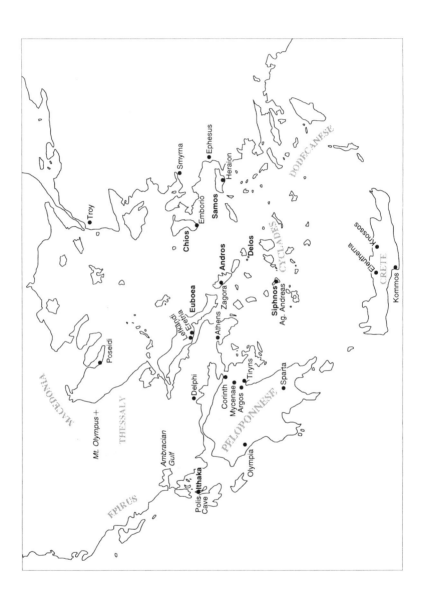

Fig. 37 Map of Dark Age Greece with principal sites.

Dorians

One of the most persistent traditions in Classical literature is that the Dorians entered the Peloponnese some time after the Trojan War, drove out the existing population, and established themselves in the whole area from the Gulf of Corinth to Crete. Thucydides (Book I, 12, 1-3) relates that they came eighty years after the Trojan War under the leadership of the *Heraklidae* (descendants of Herakles), who were *returning* to the Peloponnese. At this distance in time, it is impossible to guess whether he had specific information or, more likely, was rationalising the myths of the *nostoi* (return of the heroes from Troy). He saw this as a period of *stasis* (revolution and civil unrest). Homer, on the other hand, makes only one reference to the Dorians, already established in Crete alongside Achaeans, Eteocretans, Cydonians and Pelasgians (*Odyssey* XIX, 175-177, provided this is not an interpolation). Herodotus and others tell us that they had already moved around in Thessaly and north-western Greece before this migration (I, 56). Although the ancient sources do not convey any impression of a single migration of large numbers of people, the idea of a 'Dorian invasion', implicitly a single revolutionary event, has become embedded in recent discussions of the end of Mycenaean civilization or accounts of early Greek history.

The evidence of the Greek dialects provides the clearest indication of changes in the population of Greece during the Dark Age. By the Classical period the nearest surviving dialect to the Mycenaean form of Greek used in the Linear B script was that of Arcadia, isolated in the uplands of the central Peloponnese. A remarkably similar dialect was also used in part of Cyprus and is thought to reflect the arrival there of numbers of Mycenaean Greeks at the end of the 13th century. In NW Greece and around the coast of the Peloponnese from Elis to Sparta and the Corinthia, Dorians and 'West Greeks' formed a linguistic group which was distinct both from Arcadian and from the Ionian and other 'East Greek' dialects found from Thessaly to Attica and in Asia Minor (see below). There is no shortage of epigraphic and literary evidence from as early as the Archaic period to confirm these divisions, while differences of language and tradition also lie behind the polarisation of Greece, in the period after the Persian wars, into groups dominated by Sparta and Athens respectively. Current linguistic theory suggests, firstly, that the two dialects developed during a period of isolation from each other and, secondly, that Ionic Greek is closer to the early form used in the Linear B tablets than Doric Greek, though not perhaps as close as

Arcadian. The Athenians thought of themselves as autochthonous (native) and of the Spartans as immigrants.

Language and tradition are important sources of evidence but they provide no firm information about *when* these dialects became established in each area, nor any precision about the regions from where they came. So far archaeological research has revealed nothing which can be linked with certainty to the Dorians. Indeed, if they originated within the Mycenaean world and already shared the material culture of the Mycenaeans or their descendants, they may never be recognisable in the archaeological record.

Date BC		Principal events in Greece	Principal sites and discoveries		Principal events elsewhere
1200		Palaces destroyed			Troy VII
	L		Lefkandi	L	Ramesses III
1190	A	Iron in use	Phylakopi shrines	B	Sea Peoples
	T	Decline	Warrior Vase	A	
1100	E				
1050		Cremation common	Athens-Kerameikos		
		Iron widespread			
1000			Lefkandi 'Heroon'		Phoenician trade
	G	Re-establishment	Toumba cemetery	I	
900	E	of trade	Knossos cemeteries	R	
	O			O	Old Smyrna
	M		Athens-Areopagos	N	Pithecussai
	E		grave		
800	T		Ithaca-Polis tripods		Al Mina
776	R	Olympic Games	Zagora, Emborio	A	
	I		Eleutherna	G	Colonization
	C	? Homer ?	Argos Panoply	E	Cypriot Salamis
		Greek alphabet			
700					

Fig. 38 Dark Age Greece: Events, sites and parallels 1200-700 BC.

The palace destructions

The enormous effort behind the construction of the Mycenaean citadel walls in the 13th century BC, the provision of protected access to a water supply, and a wall across the Isthmus of Corinth which may date to the same time, may have been a response to a real threat from outsiders or from fellow Mycenaeans. If so, these great works failed in their purpose. By 1200 BC the palaces had been destroyed by fire and the complex administrative systems had vanished. There is nothing to show who or what was responsible. Theories range from invasion by hostile forces, such as the Dorians from the north or the Sea Peoples who attacked Egypt at the end of the 13th century BC, to social and economic collapse as a consequence of civil war, agricultural failure or climatic change. The causes are likely to be complex, but the consequences are clear.

Aftermath

After the destructions, there was no attempt to rebuild the palaces at Mycenae or Pylos, while only a small megaron was built on the ruins of the old one at Tiryns. No writing, on clay tablets or on pottery, has so far been found in the following period, and the citadels seem to be neither centres for storage nor manufacture. Other sites appear to be abandoned or much reduced in size. In general there was a reduction in the level of population, though it is not clear whether this was absolute or whether the inhabitants of the towns scattered to smaller villages.

The new weapon and ornament types with European parallels, which become popular after these destructions, all fit into the pattern of trade continuing in the Adriatic. Some types can already be detected before the destructions, including the presence of an unexpected kind of pottery, hand-made rather than wheel-thrown, burnished not painted and fired in a low-temperature kiln. Parallels have been suggested for this in Troy, Epirus and southern Italy, but it is nowhere more than a tiny percentage of the total amount of pottery made, and seems likely to be a symptom of social change rather than a symbol of new rulers.

Limited recovery followed and lasted about a hundred years during which the non-palatial characteristics of Mycenaean civilization continued unchanged. Some distinctive objects, such as the Warrior Vase found by Schliemann (cf. Fig. 40, p. 135), show that skills and imagination had not been lost entirely.

The Iron Age

In the final phases of Mycenaean civilization more changes can be seen, together with a further decline in prosperity, including the loss of Adriatic trade. In Athens and at Lefkandi in Euboea, single graves in new cemeteries replace the family chamber tombs used for centuries. New ornaments of simple bronze wire, long pins and arched fibulae (brooches) accompany the dead, perhaps indicating some change in fashion. Three innovations, the regular use of iron for ornaments and weapons and the practice of cremation for the dead were introduced in Athens a few years later, around 1050 BC, together with a new style of pottery decoration known as Proto-Geometric. These mark the start of the period usually known as the Iron Age. They are not changes, however, which immediately affect other parts of Greece. One of the features of this period was the variety of burial practices in use in different areas at the same time and the wide variety of pottery styles, each representing a distinct local preference. The obvious fragmentation of the late Mycenaean period, region by region, continued up to the Classical period.

The significance of **iron working** is uncertain. When iron first appears in Greece in the 17th century BC it is a very rare import, without doubt a prestige material, just as in the Near East where the Hittites jealously controlled its manufacture. The partial disintegration of the Hittite empire at the same time as the Mycenaean palatial system collapsed allowed the technology to be learnt in other areas, such as Palestine and Cyprus. It is likely that the small number of utilitarian items, chiefly knives, found in Greece in the 12th century BC, were imports from Cyprus, but no longer of outstanding value. Around 1050 BC, the techniques reached the southern Aegean and a wide range of iron items were made, almost to the exclusion of bronze. With the disappearance of the trade in copper and tin, iron was for a time the only locally available metal for practical use that could be mined in quantity. The low grade iron-ores found in Greece need considerable amounts of fuel and effort to produce usable metal, as well as technology that is so different from that of bronze working that it must only have been mastered slowly. Its use for ornaments for a short period from the mid-eleventh to the end of the tenth century BC, when they were again made in bronze, suggests that it was necessity rather than improvement that brought about the use of iron. There is no certainty that iron weapons, which at first were made in forms used for bronze, were an improvement, until the Archaic period. The first attempts to work iron may only have produced brittle objects which were neither resilient nor kept their edge. Hesiod writing in the 7th century BC regarded the 'Age of Iron' as a come-down from past glory.

Cremation may also be a practice introduced from Cyprus, but it had been used sporadically in the late Mycenaean period, in Attica, in the Argolid and in Elis in western Greece. Its adoption by whole communities was, however, erratic. Only in Athens was there a clear break from the old traditions, but even here the same cemetery, in the Kerameikos district, continued in use. After the body and some of the offerings had been burnt on a pyre, the fragments of charred bone and offerings were collected up and placed in a large clay jar, usually an amphora, in a small grave-pit with additional objects of metal or pottery. At Lefkandi, where cremation pyres have been found, the remains were placed in a full-sized grave with the objects arranged as if the body were present. At Argos, cremation did not come into fashion for more than a hundred years, a pattern to be seen in many other areas. Cremation may be an indication of increased prosperity, since the collection of sufficient timber for fuel in an area like Athens will have been a far more laborious task than digging a simple pit in the ground. There is, however, little sign of the lavish offerings and great ceremony which accompanied the cremation of such Achaean heroes as Patroclus (*Iliad* XXIII).

Pottery with Proto-Geometric style decoration, the third innovation, seems to have been used first in Athens and Cyprus, more or less simultaneously, and then spread to neighbouring areas in an erratic manner. Its hallmark is the use of a multiple brush, mounted on a compass, used to paint neat concentric circles or semicircles on a wide variety of pots. These vessels, however, though better formed and fired, are the direct descendants of those made by the previous generations of Mycenaean potters. Some shapes such as the stirrup jar are lost and some are recent novelties, such as curious bird-shaped vases, also known from Cyprus. Clearly there is a new enthusiasm in the potters' workshops, suggesting a new prosperity among their customers, but to call this a radical change, as used to be the case, seems far-fetched.

The problem which arises, when the evidence of tradition and archaeology are set side by side, is that the changes in the material culture can be seen first in the very area where continuity of population is supposed to have been strongest – Athens – and that continuity can be seen most clearly in the areas where the Dorian newcomers are supposed to have settled – western Greece. Here there are continuing distinctive traits of pottery decoration to be seen in Ithaca, Achaea and Messenia, which descend directly from their Mycenaean predecessors, with no sign of the Athenian Proto-Geometric style. Cremation is largely unknown in this area. The only correlation which can be made with tradition is that the separation of Greece into eastern and western groups is already apparent at the beginning of the Iron Age, c. 1050 BC.

The first hundred years of the Iron Age show a level of contact and economic activity little improved from that of the final stages of the

Mycenaean period. So little is known, however, of this period that each new excavation can dramatically change our perspective.

The Ionian Migration

A second population movement is recorded in the tradition and attested by the links between the dialects of Eastern mainland Greece (Attic, Thessalian etc) and those of the Asia Minor coast (Aeolic and Ionic). It took place after the Dorian arrival in the Peloponnese but cannot be dated any more precisely. The language of the Homeric epics is Ionic with Aeolic elements and the poetic tradition is usually assumed to have been brought to Asia Minor as part of this migration. No clear correlation can yet be made with archaeological evidence, but the Athenian Proto-Geometric style of pottery did appear at Miletus and other sites in the area soon after it was introduced to Attica in the 11th century.

The 'Heröon' at Lefkandi in Euboea

Towards the middle of the 10th century BC, a monumental building was erected on a hill overlooking the sea, about 1km. from the site of the Bronze Age settlement at Lefkandi. Thirty-five metres long and twelve wide, it is as large as any of the 8th-century BC temples and larger than any building since the Mycenaean palaces. Its *apsidal* form (with one curved end) is known from smaller buildings, both earlier and later, but for this period it is unique.

The finds made within it, below the floor, are equally unusual. One burial pit contained the cremated remains of a man wrapped in a linen garment and placed in a bronze jar, with hunting scenes in repoussé on the rim. Beside the jar was *inhumed* (buried unburnt) the body of a woman with gold ornaments on her breasts, long iron pins on her shoulders and a damaged gold pendant with granulation work at her neck. This pendant was part of a necklace of beads, including two glass beads of a Mycenaean type not made since the 12th century BC. Parallels for both the vessel and the pendant are best found in 12th-century BC Cyprus and this, together with the beads, suggest that these items were heirlooms treasured for several generations. It is possible that the woman was also an offering in the grave, a companion for the next life, as, surely, were the pair of horses slaughtered and buried in an adjacent pit.

The building, with stone footings, mud-brick walls and a wooden colonnade surrounding it, was intentionally demolished to form a mound of debris, which has given the name of 'Toumba' to the area. Unfortunately it is not possible to tell which came first, the building or the burial. Was this a chief's house used as his burial place and then demolished to cover it? Alternatively, was the building erected specifically to house the burial, a kind of *heröon* in honour of the dead? Whichever the case, the mound had already been heaped up by the end of the century and became a focus for a new cemetery – the 'Toumba cemetery' – with rich offerings, perhaps of the chief's immediate descendants and clan.

Renewed trade and expansion

With the exception of Crete, where some form of contact with Cyprus and the Near East was maintained throughout the transition from Bronze to Iron Age, the remainder of Greece was largely isolated, both district from district and from wider Mediterranean commerce. The first indications of a renewal of contact at the end of the 10th century BC are seen at Lefkandi, and particularly in the Toumba cemetery. Here there is not only gold jewellery in quantity, together with imported pottery from Athens, Thessaly and even Macedonia, but an extra-ordinary number of items of Egyptian and Near Eastern origin. These include a bronze bucket with Egyptian scenes incised on it, several small jugs with handles ending in schematic lotus flowers, faience bottles modelled as bunches of grapes and other forms, faience scarabs, seals and rings, including one with a ram's head and sun disc – the emblems of the Egyptian god Amun. These are surely burials of 'merchants' who were once again trading in the Eastern Mediterranean, with the Egyptians and the Phoenicians. (The famous Phoenician cities of the Levant coast, such as Tyre and Sidon, had survived the incursions of the Sea Peoples, to become great commercial centres.) At the contemporary settlement at Lefkandi, the renewal of technological skills can be seen in the fragments of clay moulds used for casting bronze tripod legs, such as those frequently found in sanctuaries (see p. 129).

Soon after, in the 9th century BC, this wealth can be seen to have spread to Athens. The burial on the Areopagus hill of a rich woman contained a superb pair of granulated gold earrings, six gold finger rings, a necklace of over a thousand glass beads imported from the Near East, a model granary and fifty-five pottery vessels, as well as many other objects. Argos, which had replaced Mycenae and Tiryns as the leading community of the Argolid, also shared in this prosperity. Lead and silver slags show that smelting and refining for the extraction of silver took place at the same period. Elsewhere progress seems slower, though this may partly be due to gaps in the archaeological record. It is curious, for example, that Corinth which soon came to prominence as a trading community has not yet revealed any rich graves at this date.

By the beginning of the 8th century the overseas activity of the Corinthians and the Euboeans can be seen clearly in the distribution of pottery in Italy from both areas and, in Phoenicia, predominantly from Euboea. Two places of particular importance in the development of trade were Al Mina, at the mouth of the Orontes river, and Pithecoussai on the island of Ischia near Naples. The Greeks were not yet ready for the colonial movement of the second half of the 8th century when their aim was settlement as much as trade, but a period of exploration and trade clearly preceded this colonisation by two or three generations. As in the Bronze Age, it may have been the metals trade that provided the impetus. Much Corinthian pottery has been found in burials in north central Italy, within reach of the copper-ore sources of that area.

Settlements

Information about Iron Age settlements is minimal until the beginning of the 8th century BC, perhaps because later building and construction has removed most of the evidence. A number of 8th-century sites do illustrate their character: Zagora on Andros, Agios Andreas on Siphnos, and Emborio on Chios. These were settlements of short duration and soon abandoned. They have fortification walls, clusters of simple stone-built houses, and larger buildings at their centre. At Old Smyrna on the western coast of Turkey, massive fortifications of stone and mud-brick enclosed a large plateau.

A new heroic age

The start of formal colonisation around 750 BC marks a new heroic age, approximately the 'Late Geometric' period, when rulers and warriors aspired to the status of their ancestors and spared no expense in life or death. In Athens, huge vases – kraters for men and amphorae for women – served as grave markers for cremation burials and were often elaborately decorated with scenes of funerary processions. In Argos, a rich grave contained a bronze cuirass and helmet, a pair of iron fire-dogs or spit stands in the shape of galleys, and twelve iron spits, as well as pottery and items of gold. At Eleutherna in Crete, a cremation cemetery contained rich burials with bronze cauldrons for the ashes. One of the most elaborate cremations seems to have been accompanied by the ritual slaughter of a young man in the manner described by Homer for the funeral of Patroclus (*Iliad* XIII, 175-177). In Euboea, at Eretria (10km. south of, and perhaps the successor town to, Lefkandi), more rich cremation burials in bronze cauldrons and a hoard of scrap gold attest the continuing wealth of the area. Further away at Salamis in Cyprus, the Homeric echoes are even stronger. Here, at a city with strong Euboean connections, which according to legend was founded by Teucer after the Trojan War, are a series of rock-cut tombs with monumental facades. These contained the cremation burials of rich aristocrats with the remains of horses and even servants slaughtered in the dromoi, together with chariots and harness, pots of olive oil or honey (as provided for Patroclus), precious jewellery and much Euboean pottery of Geometric style.

A clear reflection of heroic deeds can be seen in several of the decorated vases of the period. On one vase a man leads a woman carrying a bridal wreath on to a many-oared galley. On another, a man sits on the upturned hull of a boat while apparently drowned men float in the water around it (Fig. 39, p. 133). Unlike many later vases there are as yet no 'captions' to identify these scenes, but it does not take much imagination to link them with Paris' abduction of Helen or Odysseus surviving shipwreck by clinging to the hull of his boat.

Sanctuaries

Dozens of sanctuaries are known all over Greece at this period, on hill-tops, in caves or at sites of major importance such as Delphi and Delos, Olympia, Samos and Ephesus. Some of these sanctuaries were used from at least the 10th century BC, and some must have had a connection with the cult places of the Mycenaean period. At present the best evidence for continuity of cult can be found at Kommos, on the south coast of Crete, and at Poseidi in Chalcidike, where somehow the memory of a sanctuary of Poseidon survived in the toponym, even though its very existence was only recently recognised. Only in the 8th century BC, however, do new offerings express the renewed prosperity of Greece, most clearly seen in the sheer quantities of bronze dedications in these sanctuaries. Bronze jewellery and figurines of humans, horses and other animals, bronze spears and shield fittings, are commonplace, but the most striking of all the offerings are the massive cast legs of the great bronze tripod stands which are familiar as gifts from one Homeric prince to another, or as prizes at athletic contests like those held in honour of Patroclus.

At first these sanctuaries did not need more than an open-air altar, but gradually the custom arose of building a temple, itself a dedication to the patron divinity. At Eretria there is an 8th-century BC temple to Apollo, of apsidal form, though much smaller than the Heröon at Lefkandi. Models of this kind of temple have been found at Perachora near Corinth and at the Argive Heraion, the principal sanctuary to Hera in the Argolid. They are small buildings with pitched roofs and a shallow colonnaded porch in front of the door. Other early temple buildings are known at the Artemision at Ephesus, at the Heraion on the island of Samos, at Isthmia near Corinth and on the island of Naxos.

Homer and the monuments

It would be nice to know exactly when Homer lived, or indeed how many poets he (or she) was. However, following the Classical tradition, the *Iliad* and the *Odyssey* and the other epic works, of which scraps only survive, had reached their final form as oral poetry by the early Archaic period in the 7th century BC. They were then transmitted, it is presumed, with only minor changes, in the bardic tradition of the *Homeridae*, a guild of performers who recited parts of the poems at festivals or private feasts. At some disputed point, perhaps in Athens under the rule of Peisistratos, a written form emerged. It is certain, from the archaeological evidence of the heroic burials and the painted pottery, that the stories were popular in the late 8th century BC. They were re-sung, in instalments, time after time to eager audiences at least until the 4th century BC, much as the blind bard Demodocus entertained the lords in Phaeacia (*Odyssey* VIII, 40-108). It must not be forgotten that although the epics are good stories, their purpose was also didactic and the links between unjust or impious action and retribution, human or divine, are clearly made. Some of the detail and some of the similes – where reflections of a particular period seem to be most obvious – were carefully chosen by the poet to reflect the base or the noble, not as an historical record.

Another area of uncertainty is the priority of the epic or the archaeology. When does the epic reflect past practices (anything up to 800 years earlier) or when do contemporary practices reflect the epic? To give one simple example, fragments of thirteen bronze tripod stands of 9th- or 8th- century date were found in the Polis cave on Ithaca. This cave, used from the Mycenaean period, was the most likely spot for the Phaeacians to have left Odysseus asleep on the beach and for him to be bidden by Athena to hide his treasure in a nearby cave (*Odyssey* XIII, 363-371). Although not of the Mycenaean period, were these, in truth, the tripods a Dark Age Odysseus hid and failed to collect or, more plausibly, were they provided at some date later than Odysseus' return to support the famous story? Heroic/Homeric characteristics continued to be cultivated in this way in later generations. The third-century BC cenotaph of Nicocreon, King of Salamis in Cyprus, with its pyre and funeral offerings, consciously echoes the burial rites of Patroclus.

Working backwards from the 8th century BC and trying to unravel the woven tapestry of the myth and reality of different periods is a truly Sisyphean task. It is beyond doubt that there was a continuous process of alteration of, and addition to, the stories, from those first remote times when they were inspired, to their final consolidation in the written form of the Greek epic in hexameter verse.

Three periods, however, are the most likely to have been crucial in the formation of the epic stories, though the argument about which was the most important is unending. The first appearance of Homer's Achaeans on the stage of history could be set in the period of the Shaft Graves, when powerful rulers were buried with great ceremony at Mycenae. The second possibility is at the height of Mycenaean power, when Cyclopean fortifications were built and trade extended throughout the Mediterranean. The third, though less likely, is during the early Dark Age when on a smaller, local stage petty chieftains may have competed with each other for supremacy.

Many aspects of Mycenaean art in the Shaft Grave period reflect the theme of an expedition against a city like Troy. The silver Siege Rhyton from Grave Circle A at Mycenae shows attackers below and defenders on the walls of a well-built citadel. The contemporary Ship Fresco from the West House at Akrotiri shows a flotilla of ships and towns with onlookers and defenders. Does this depict the kind of military expedition reflected by the story of Troy, or a peaceful festival? Other items in use at the beginning of the Mycenaean period seem familiar from the epic. The famous boar's tusk helmet, already an heirloom when given by Amphidamus to Molus in exchange for hospitality, and later by Molus's son Meriones to Odysseus (*Iliad* X, 266-70), is the best known example. If this is the correct date for the origin of the epic, then the anachronistic detail, such as lavish cremation burial, must be regarded as later accretion during the process of transmission.

Indeed, there are those who hold not only that the epic stories derive from the Shaft Grave period but that they are based on the survival of Mycenaean poetry. In this view (hard to reconcile with the form of the language of the epic hexameters) Homer was himself a Mycenaean poet. Others, more cautiously, regard the kernel of the story, the Trojan War and The Return of Odysseus and other heroes, as generally Bronze Age in origin but with the final form developing late, so that all the echoes of different periods were melded into the near perfect whole which survives today. This view sees Homer's lifetime in the Late Geometric period and the rather artificial form of language as perhaps a conscious archaism.

If the key element in the story is the union of most of Greece in a great expedition, the only conceivable period for the siege of Troy is that of the 13th century BC when Mycenaean power was at its height. The places listed in the 'catalogue of ships' bear a surprising resemblance to the principal Mycenaean sites of that period known from excavation. Boar's tusk helmets were still in use; fragments of wall-painting from Mycenae show a soldier falling from a city wall and at Pylos Mycenaean forces battled with skin-clad 'foreigners'.

The *Iliad* and the *Odyssey* do not necessarily reflect the same eras to the same extent. The theme of the returning heroes may be Mycenaean but the troubles they face on their return suggest the aftermath of the collapse of the Mycenaean Palaces. The certainties of the heroic age have been swept aside by the time Odysseus himself returns to reassert his authority. For the same reason, it seems less probable that the story of the siege of Troy originated during this period.

Some elements, subsidiary to the main stories, are surely of Dark Age origin. References to Phoenician silver bowls belong to the 9th century BC and, indeed, there is one from Knossos of that date with a Phoenician inscription on it. Not only is the use of iron quite frequent but the very technology which Hephaistos uses to make the bronze armour for Achilles is that of the black-smith, not the bronze-smith (*Iliad* XVIII, 468-477). He throws the metal (even if it is described as bronze, with tin, gold and silver) on the fire, heated by twenty (automatic!) bellows, and prepares to hammer it hot on an anvil with tongs to hold it. Bronze is cast and, like copper, worked *cold*. Only *iron* is worked at white heat with a hammer to shape it.

The other major theme of the *Odyssey*, the ten years of exile and adventure, has also been seen as chiefly the product of a later age. Essentially, the *Odyssey* belongs to the vast genre of travellers' tales. Just as the stories of Sinbad the sailor are the product of the first adventures of the Arabs into the perils of the Indian Ocean and those of Columbus' contemporaries reflect the discovery of the New World, so those of Odysseus surely reflect a period of exploration. Should this be set as early as the Shaft Graves when the first signs of Mycenaean traders are found in the Western Mediterranean (where perhaps they met with Scylla and Charybdis in the currents of the straits of Messina between Italy and Sicily)? Is it, alternatively, a product of the 9th century BC, when, for the first time in two centuries, Greek seafarers regularly ventured westwards across the Adriatic – and perhaps embellished their stories of the dangers to deter competitors? It can be no accident that Ithaca, with its sheltered harbours, the natural first and last port of call on this leap into the unknown, was the legendary home of the intrepid Odysseus, or that for centuries to come travellers would dedicate offerings in his honour, or to win his protection, at the Ithacan sanctuaries of Polis and Aetos. The *Odyssey* also provides many more clues about contemporary society than the *Iliad*. Does Odysseus represent the all-powerful king of Ithaca, or was he, as often in later centuries, one of a group of rival aristocrats holding power precariously by force of arms and strength of wit?

Well over two-and-a-half thousand years have passed since the composition of the epics. Barely a twentieth of this time has elapsed since Schliemann's persistence – in excavation and in argument – convinced other scholars that there was a tangible foundation to the stories. Today the question is not whether Mycenaean warriors were Homer's Achaean heroes, but where to set the line between fact and fiction. Barring a miraculous discovery among the papyri of Egypt, the epic will remain unchanged but every year new archaeological discoveries add to, or modify, our picture of the Mycenaean world and the Dark Age that followed. The match between the Homeric legend and the archaeological reality is constantly shifting. Even if we could agree between ourselves today, by tomorrow – let alone the next millennium – our story will need to be retold.

Fig. 39 Odysseus Shipwrecked: on Late Geometric vase, c. 725 BC.

Suggestions for Further Study

Each of you will doubtless have your own views about where the Homeric epics fit against this background of archaeological fact and speculation. First try to understand the pattern of the discoveries (1-6) and only then look for their reflection in the epic (7-9). Read the epics again and again, both for their own sake and to try to understand and recreate for yourselves the societies which produced them.

1. Look at the illustrated books you can find – site guides, museum catalogues etc – and see what variety of jewellery, objects of bronze or ivory were made by Mycenaean craftsmen.

2. Compare the dress and ornaments shown on the Thera wall-paintings with those found on the Greek mainland and with objects found in the Shaft graves at Mycenae. How far do they differ?

3. Compare objects found in mainland Greece with those from Minoan Crete. How do they differ or how far do they represent a single civilization? (Your opinion, based on the evidence, is as valid as anybody else's!)

4. Use a map of the Mediterranean area to mark the find-spots of Mycenaean pottery and other objects you have learnt about in your reading – and the sources of raw materials which they used. Can you trace any of Odysseus' voyages in this area?

5. If you have copies of Chadwick's *Mycenaean World* or his *Linear B and related scripts*, make yourselves clay tablets and use a pointed tool to copy some of the ideograms and words. Study the systems of counting and make up your own records of transactions. You will have a much better understanding of the duties of a Mycenaean scribe when you have finished. (You can use pen and ink, but it is less fun...)

6. Visit one of the museums with a collection of Mycenaean artefacts and look at each category (pottery, metal, stone etc) carefully. How far can the purpose of each be determined? Where did the raw materials for each come from? Where were they made and where were they found? What information does this provide about the extent and importance of Mycenaean contact with neighbouring areas?

7. Read Homer's *Odyssey* (again) and collect information about the palaces of the Phaeacian king and of Odysseus etc. How far does this compare with what you know about Mycenaean Greece?

8. Read the *Iliad* to collect information about weapons and armour. How much of these resemble the Mycenaean examples which have been found in graves and other places?

9. Consider the main elements of the Trojan War story. Which do you consider to be 'historical' and which would you relate to Mycenaean Greece?

10. Plan a tour of Greece to visit Mycenaean sites and museums with good Mycenaean collections; decide what you particularly want to see and why.

11. Do it.

Fig. 40 'The beginning of the Dark Age?' Cartoon by Henry Hankey.

Suggestions for Further Reading

Although there has been a vast amount written about the Mycenaeans and their civilization and many of the monuments and objects they created have been illustrated in a wealth of picture and guide books, there are very few recent standard works of reference available. Thus any list of suggested reading can only be an indication of what to look out for, in public libraries or second-hand book shops, supplemented by the excellent guide books for many sites and museums to be bought through Old Vicarage Publications, Zeno Booksellers, Hellenic Bookservices or during visits to Greece itself. Although theories about the Mycenaeans have changed over the years and chronology has become more accurate, the descriptions of sites and objects remain invaluable, however old. Specialist study of any topic will probably require access to a University library (or the Library of the Society for Promotion of Hellenic Studies), where series such as the *Annual of the British School at Athens* (*BSA*), the *American Journal of Archaeology* (*AJA*) or *Studies in Mediterranean Archaeology* are available. For those with access to the Internet, there is a steadily increasing number of sites to be visited and images to be downloaded but care should be taken to check that the site 'owner' is a reputable college or institution. Teachers or undergraduates wishing to study in Greece should apply for admission to the British School at Athens and its excellent library.

Initial further reading, likely to be found in many libraries

Brief standard introductions to the **Greek Bronze Age** include P.M. Warren's *The Aegean Civilizations* (Phaidon 1975, 2nd edn. 1990) and K.A. Wardle 'The Minoan and Mycenaean Palace Societies' in B. Cunliffe, *The Oxford Illustrated Prehistory of Europe* (OUP 1994). Popular illustrated accounts of the period include J. Hawkes, *The Dawn of the Gods* (Chatto and Windus 1968), R. Higgins, *Minoan and Mycenaean Art*, (Thames and Hudson 1981) and M.S.F. Hood, *The Arts in Prehistoric Greece* (Pelican History of Art 1968), while the best illustrations of objects (apart from those in guide books and catalogues) are to be found in Sp. Marinatos and M. Hirmer, *Crete and Mycenae* (Thames and Hudson 1960) reprinted with additions as *Crete, Mycenae and Thera* (1973) and G.A. Christopoulos (ed) *History of the Hellenic World I: prehistory and protohistory* (Ekdotike Athenon 1974). R.V. Schoder, *Ancient Greece from the Air* (Thames and Hudson 1974) provides useful illustrations of the setting of prehistoric as well as Classical sites.

Books specifically on the **Mycenaeans** include M.S. Hood, *The Home of the Heroes: the Aegean before the Greeks* (Thames and Hudson 1967), Lord W. Taylour, *The Mycenaeans* (Thames and Hudson 1964, 1983), F.H. Stubbings, *Prehistoric Greece* (Hart-Davis 1972) and G. Mylonas' *Mycenae Rich in Gold* (Ekdotike Athenon 1983) with its lavish colour illustrations. J. Chadwick, *The Mycenaean World* (CUP 1976) and J.T. Hooker, *Mycenaean Greece* (Routledge 1977) are both especially important for relating the Linear B archives to the archaeological evidence, while Chadwick's *Linear B and related scripts* (British Museum 1987) provides a useful introduction. L.R. Palmer's *Mycenaeans and Minoans* (Faber and Faber 1961, 1965) is still a valuable source of alternative interpretations of the texts, a reminder of how much is still a matter of debate.

The extent to which Homeric poetry is Mycenaean is discussed by E.S. Sherratt in 'Reading the texts: archaeology and the Homeric question' in *Antiquity* 64 1990, 807-24. Two older books, H. Lorimer, *Homer and the Monuments* (Macmillan 1950) and A.J.B. Wace and F.H. Stubbings, *A Companion to Homer* (Macmillan 1963) still provide invaluable discussions of Homeric parallels, though some now need to be updated or emended. A more recent study of the same topic can be found in J.V. Luce, *Homer and the Heroic Age* (Thames and Hudson 1975). M. Wood's study of the period in *In Search of the Trojan War* (BBC 1985) is intended for a popular market but goes much deeper than this. It includes many recent discoveries, and asks several searching questions.

Those wishing to understand the nature of the relationship between Mycenaean Greece and the other peoples of the Central and Eastern Mediterranean will find N.K. Sandars, *The Sea Peoples* (Thames and Hudson 1978, 1985) a valuable introduction, even though its main focus is on the period around 1200 BC when there were upheavals throughout Anatolia, the Levant and coastal Egypt.

Minoan archaeology is equally well served by such studies as: G. Cadogan, *Palaces of Minoan Crete*, (Methuen 1980), which focusses on the sites, or R. Higgins, *The Archaeology of Minoan Crete* (Bodley Head 1973) and M.S.F. Hood, *The Minoans* (Thames and Hudson 1971) which provide more illustrations of Cretan artefacts. Ch. Doumas, *Thera, Pompeii of the ancient Aegean* (Thames and Hudson 1983) provides a clear summary of the principal finds at Akrotiri.

Most **site publications** are only accessible in University libraries but Heinrich Schliemann's studies of *Mycenae* (1880, reprinted Arno 1976), *Tiryns* (1885, reprinted Arno 1976) and Troy (*Troy*, 1875, *Ilios* 1880, *Troja* 1884, all reprinted Arno 1976) are widely available and include useful 'first hand' information. C.W. Blegen, *Troy and the Trojans* (Thames and Hudson 1963) puts Troy in its context, while Mylonas (above) does the same for Mycenae. C.W. Blegen and M. Rawson's *A Guide to the Palace of Nestor*, (Cincinnati 1967) gives a brief summary of this important site. Note also that *Archaeological Reports* published jointly by the Society for Promotion of Hellenic Studies and the British School at Athens provides an annual review of new discoveries of all periods.

A number of books provide studies of aspects of the **Dark Age**. M. Finley's *World of Odysseus* (Penguin 1972, and Chatto and Windus 1977) should be readily available while R. Osborne's recent study of early Greece, *Greece in the Making 1200-479 BC* (Routledge 1996), is invaluable for the insights it provides into the Archaic period when myths were as much created as transmitted.

Internet sites

J. Rutter of Dartmouth College has made his teaching notes and full bibliographies on the *Prehistoric Archaeology of the Aegean* available at **http://devlab.cs.dartmouth.edu/history/bronze_age/** and a forum for presentation of new discoveries can be found on the *Aegeanet* at **http://www.umich.edu/~classics/archives/aegeanet/**

There is a vast range of information about the ancient world at **http://perseus.csad.ox.ac.uk/** and another site with links to a wide range of topics is located at **http://www.duke.edu/web/jyounger/kapat96.html**

The authors will also do their best to maintain an up-to-date index of useful websites at **http://www.bham.ac.uk/aha/aegeaninfo/** The Greek Ministry of Culture's own website with details of museums and ancient sites can be accessed at **http://www.culture.gr/** The British School at Athens site is at **http://www.bsa.gla.ac.uk/main.html** and that of the Society for Promotion of Hellenic Studies at **http://www.sas.ac.uk/icls/Hellenic/**

A small selection of more detailed studies, likely to be found in University Libraries:

Chapter 2. The rise and fall of Mycenaean civilization

O.T.P.K. Dickinson, *The Aegean Bronze Age* (Cambridge 1994) – excellent bibliography.

O.T.P.K. Dickinson, *The Origins of Mycenaean Civilization* (Göteborg 1977).

O.T.P.K. Dickinson and R. Hope Simpson, *A gazetteer of Aegean civilisation in the Bronze Age. – Vol.1: The Mainland.* (Göteborg 1979).

J. Driessen and C.F. MacDonald, *The troubled island: Minoan Crete before and after the Santorini eruption* (Liège 1997).

J.W. Myers, E.E. Myres and G. Cadogan, *Aerial Atlas of Ancient Crete* (Univ. California Press and London 1992).

C.W. Shelmerdine, 'Review of Aegean Prehistory VI: The Palatial Bronze Age of the Southern and Central Greek Mainland', *AJA* 101 (1997) 537-85.

Chapter 3. Cities

C.W. Blegen, J.L. Caskey and M.Rawson, *Troy III: The Sixth Settlement* (Princeton 1953).

C.W. Blegen and M. Rawson, *The Palace of Nestor at Pylos in Western Messenia I: The buildings and and their contents* (Princeton 1966).

P.A. Mountjoy, *Mycenaean Athens* (Jonsered 1995).

J. Pendlebury, *Palace of Minos* (London 1954).

S. Symeonoglou, *The Topography of Thebes from the Bronze Age to Modern Times* (Princeton 1985).

A.J.B. Wace, *Mycenae: an Archaeological History and Guide* (Princeton 1949).

Chapter 4. Tombs and burial practices

O.T.P.K. Dickinson, 'Cist Graves and Chamber Tombs', *BSA* 78 (1983) 55-67.

R. Hägg and N. Marinatos (eds.), *Celebrations of Death and Divinity in the Bronze Age Argolid* (Stockholm 1990).

C.B. Mee and W.G. Cavanagh, *A private place: death in prehistoric Greece* (Jonsered 1998).

C. B. Mee and W.G. Cavanagh, 'The Spatial Distribution of Mycenaean Tombs', *BSA* 85 (1990) 225-243.

Chapter 5. Materials and technology

O.H. Krzyszkowska, *Ivory and Related Materials* (London 1990).

R. Laffineur and P.P. Betancourt (eds.), *TEXNH: Craftsmen, Craftswomen and Craftsmanship in the Aegean Bronze Age* (Liège 1997).

Chapter 6. Economy and society

P. Halstead, 'The Development of Agriculture and Pastoralism in Greece' in D.R. Harris (ed.), *The Origins and Spread of Agriculture and Pastoralism in Eurasia* (London 1996) 296-309.

J.T. Killen, 'The Wool Industry of Crete in the Late Bronze Age', *BSA* 59 (1964) 1-15.

T. van Andel, C. Runnels and K. Pope, 'Five Thousand Years of Land Use and Abuse in the Southern Argolid', *Hesperia* 55 (1986) 103-28.

M. Ventris and J. Chadwick, *Documents in Mycenaean Greek* (2nd edn. Cambridge 1973).

Chapter 7. Building and engineering

J.M. Balcer, 'The Mycenaean Dam at Tiryns', *AJA* 78 (1974) 141-49.

W.G. Cavanagh and R.R. Laxton, 'The Structural Mechanics of the Mycenaean Tholos Tomb', *BSA* 76 (1981) 109-40.

S. Iakovidis, *Late Helladic Citadels on Mainland Greece* (Leiden 1983).

Chapter 8. Weapons and warfare

P.Åström et al., *The Cuirass Tomb and other finds at Dendra. Part 1: The Chamber Tombs* (Göteborg 1977).

M.A. Littauer and J.H. Crouwel, 'Chariots in Late Bronze Age Greece', *Antiquity* 57 (1983) 187-92.

N.K. Sandars, 'The First Aegean Swords and their Ancestry', *AJA* 65 (1961) 17-29.

N.K. Sandars, 'Later Aegean Bronze Swords', *AJA* 67 (1963) 117-53.

Chapter 9. Wall-paintings

Chr. Doumas, *The wall-paintings of Thera* (Athens 1992).

S.A. Immerwahr, *Aegean Painting in the Bronze Age* (Pennsylvania 1990).

M.L. Lang, *The Palace of Nestor at Pylos in Western Messenia II: The Frescoes* (Princeton 1969).

L. Morgan, *The Miniature Wall Paintings of Thera: A Study in Aegean Culture and Iconography* (Cambridge 1988).

Chapter 10. Trade and contact

G.F. Bass, C. Pulak, D. Collon and J. Weinstein, 'The Bronze Age Shipwreck at Ulu Burun (Kas): 1986 Campaign', *AJA* 93 (1989) 1-29.

E.H. Cline, *Sailing the Wine-dark Sea: International Trade and the Late Bronze Age Aegean* (Oxford 1994).

N.H. Gale (ed.), *Bronze Age Trade in the Mediterranean* (Jonsered 1991).

C. and P. Zerner and J. Winder (eds.), *Wace and Blegen: Pottery as Evidence for Trade in the Aegean Bronze Age* (Amsterdam 1993).

Chapter 11. Religion

R. Hägg and N. Marinatos (eds.), *Sanctuaries and Cults in the Aegean Bronze Age* (Stockholm 1981).

A.C. Renfrew, *The Archaeology of Cult: the sanctuary at Phylakopi* (London 1985).

W.D. Taylour, E.B. French and K.A. Wardle, *Well Built Mycenae, Fasc 10: The Temple Complex* (Oxford 1999).

Chapter 12. Homer and the Dark Age

J.N. Coldstream, *Geometric Greece* (London 1977).

V.R. d'A. Desborough, *The Greek Dark Ages* (London 1972).

I. Morris, *Burial and Ancient Society, the rise of the Greek city state* (Cambridge 1987).

I. Morris, *A New Companion to Homer* (Leiden 1998).

A.M. Snodgrass, *The Dark Age of Greece* (Edinburgh 1971).

Index